GET IN THE GALLEY AND ROW

GET IN THE GALLEY AND ROW

JOHN TRIFFITT

in Christ alone.

Get in the Galley and Row

Copyright © 2019 by John Triffitt.

Published using **Book**Lab services, www.thebooklab.co.uk

No part of this book shall be reproduced or transmitted in any form or by any means, electronic or mechanical, including photocopying, recording, or by any information retrieval system without written permission from the publisher. All photographs are from the authors private collection.

All Bible quotations are from the New King James Version unless otherwise stated in the text.

ISBN: 9781674293912

INTRODUCTION TO THE SERIES

This is the second in a series of small books designed, God willing, to create a big impact. The first, *Men of Dust, Men of Glory*, was published in 2019. Each volume is written to encourage men to embrace Biblical manhood and masculinity. These are all written as practical manuals, following on from my books *Behold the Man* (co-authored with my friend, Dr Mark Stibbe), and *Freedom Fighters*.

DEDICATION

This book is dedicated to my wife and partner in the galley, Paula. When it comes to having someone below the decks serving with me for God's purposes in the earth for our generation, there is no other I'd rather have beside me. Paula, you embody the words within these pages.

ACKNOWLEDGEMENTS

I would like to express special thanks for Mark Stibbe who has an exquisite gift to help me scribe on paper what is written in my heart. I'm also deeply indebted to Jason Carter and Ian Harris for their dedication and creativity in the layout and design.

The Roman Empire was not only built by the strength of the legions, but also by a navy that was one of the most powerful maritime forces ever to have existed. It was only the existence of Rome's fleet that secured its trade routes and maintained communications within the huge Empire. At the height of its power, the Roman navy employed tens of thousands of sailors, marines, and craftsmen, coming from every corner of the three continents under the rule of the Caesars.

Raffaele D'Amato

CONTENTS

1. Getting on Board — OPPORTUNITY — 15

2. The Volunteer Spirit — BRAVERY — 31

3. Men Under Authority — HUMILITY — 49

4. No Slackers Allowed! — INDUSTRY — 63

5. Rowing in Unison — UNITY — 79

6. Minding the Gap — INTEGRITY — 93

7. Someone Above Decks — DESTINY — 111

CHAPTER 1

GETTING ON BOARD

There was once a man who thought he was going to heaven when he died until one day he found himself on board a ship in a ferocious storm. The year was 1735 and the man concerned was a Church of England clergyman on his way to the USA. As the waves rose and the winds roared, there was increasing concern on board. Even experienced sailors were becoming fearful as the gale lashed the sails and seawater drenched the decks.

The clergyman knew that his chances of survival were slim. He tried to pray, but fear assaulted his thoughts as violently as the wind. There was no peace in his soul, no serenity in the middle of the turbulence raging all about him. God seemed remote, distant, unapproachable. He tried to ask God for help, but his words would not form with any clarity or certainty. They died in his throat before they ever had a chance to leap from his mouth.

Just then, he noticed something, a group of German passengers standing on the top deck. A father, a mother, some children. All with heads bowed. They were praying. Speaking to their Heavenly Father with joy on their faces. They knew they belonged to God. They were sure that they were His children and they were even singing hymns of praise in the face of almost certain death.

In short, they looked radiant and happy while the clergyman felt forlorn, fearful and hopeless.

That moment changed everything. Not straight away. But over

time. The clergyman survived, as did the other passengers and crew, and the ship docked. For the next two years, the clergyman kept remembering the little children on board the ship, so certain they were going to heaven, so ready to meet their Maker. It provoked him constantly as he wrestled with the gap between what faith he had and what they had clearly possessed.

When the man returned to Great Britain in 1738, he found himself one night at the back of a church in London. He didn't want to be there. He was not in the best mood for a Bible study. But the speaker was reading some words from the great church reformer Martin Luther – words about how studying the first chapter of Romans had transformed Luther's life.

Suddenly, the clergyman's eyes were opened. He was later to admit, "my heart was strangely warmed." The assurance he had lacked on board the ship infused his soul, bringing with it that same peace and joy he had seen on the faces of the passengers on board the storm-whipped ship.

From then on, he travelled the length and breadth of the country, preaching the Good News that we are saved from sin and given the assurance of eternal life by believing in Jesus. He proclaimed the Good News about Jesus to a nation that was drunk on gin, served by a national church that had lost its way and its faith. The results were extraordinary.

That man heard the call, stood to his feet, climbed onto his horse, and single-handedly saved Great Britain from the terrors of the French Revolution – a fact that even secular historians are prepared to admit.

Presented with a once-in-a-lifetime opportunity, he seized it with both hands, serving God's purposes in his generation in a way that no British man has arguably ever done since.

His name?

John Wesley.

CHAPTER 1 | GETTING ON BOARD

Seizing the Day

It was Leonard Ravenhill who once said that "the opportunity of a lifetime needs to be seized in the lifetime of the opportunity." That's right. Opportunities to serve God in a culture-changing way only come to an individual when God sovereignly puts them in our path.

You must capture the moment before the moment passes!

If we're honest, much of our lives is lived in ordinary contexts doing mundane tasks. For Christian men, a great deal of our time is about being faithful to God in the small things – in serving our families, in working for a boss, in helping our neighbours, in being faithful witnesses in our recreational lives. It's not about dramatic tempests and preaching on horseback. It's about wiping down work surfaces, walking dogs and changing nappies. Most of the time, our opportunities to serve lie in the ordinary.

The Bible is so encouraging for those of us who empathise with this because it talks about two different understandings of time. There is, firstly, *mundane* time. This is every day, ordinary, run-of-the-mill time. You become conscious of it the moment your alarm clock goes off in the morning. You become conscious of it again at work as you look at your watch during the day, pausing for lunch and tea breaks. You are aware of it when you go home, when it's bedtime for the kids, when you head to bed yourself, making sure that the alarm is set for the next morning, so you can begin again your own version of what Bill Murray experiences in that brilliant comedy film, *Groundhog Day*.

It was Dave Allen, the famous comedian of the 1970s and 80s, who used to observe that most men spend their entire lives looking at the clock, from the moment they clock in at work until the moment they clock out. They do this every year for forty years and then they retire. And what does the firm give them as a retiring present? A clock!

That may highlight the difference between working practices then and now, but it also illustrates what the Bible refers to as *chronos* - chronological time. This is emphatically *mundane* time.

But, then, there's a different kind of time in the Bible. After years and years of experiencing ordinary time, a man who has proven faithful to God in the little things of life is presented with a unique opportunity. It becomes clear when that opportunity comes, that everything in his life has been building up to this moment. This is what the Bible calls *kairos* – *sacred* time. If mundane time is ordinary, human time, then sacred time is extraordinary, divine time. It is a moment in our mundane time in which God gives us a unique opportunity to do something that will have a cultural, generational impact. This is a *carpe diem* invitation – it is an invitation to "Seize the Day." There will never be another moment like this. The man of God must accept the offer to rise and do something extraordinary for God or miss it altogether and forever.

What shall we call this moment?

It is the moment when *preparation meets opportunity*.

Up to this intersection of sacred time in our mundane time, everything has been about God preparing the foundations for our life's purpose. This long season of preparation has often involved years and years of hiddenness, years and years of anonymity and invisibility.

If that's you, you're in very good company!

Think of Jesus. He spent thirty years in a construction business in his much-despised hometown of Nazareth. He was faithful in the little tasks, trusting his Heavenly Father in what the Bible calls "the days of small things." Then, after three decades of what are sometimes referred to as the "hidden" or "silent years", the call came and Jesus proclaimed that "the time had been fulfilled", that God's Kairos time had arrived (Mark 1:15). From that moment, Jesus seized the opportunity of history in the history of the opportunity. Having been faithful in the little things, the Father entrusted him with much bigger things. The greatest thing of all, in fact – the salvation of the world.

At Your Service

Let's look at another example, this time from the Old Testament - King David. What was he doing throughout his youth? It certainly wasn't wearing a crown, sitting on a throne and ruling a nation. No, he was out on the hills, serving in an unseen way as a shepherd boy. And there's nothing glamorous about that either. Let me remind you that shepherds were regarded as the lowest of the low. They were at the bottom of the social rung in Israel. Spending their time out with the sheep, they were grimy and grubby men with dirt in their fingernails and dung in their hair. If you'd been around at the time, you would probably have *smelt* them before you *saw* them. No wonder people looked down on them. No wonder Jesus, when talking about himself as a Shepherd, added the word "Good," or more accurately "Noble" (John 10). In a world where shepherds were deemed "bad" and "ignoble", Jesus needed to make this clear.

David was an extraordinary man in this regard. Before he ever ruled like a prince, he served as a peasant. Yes, I said "peasant." Shepherds were part of the *peasant class* in Israel. They were a class of workers known as the *Am Ha Aretz*, the people of the land. David therefore associated with the last and the least for a significant season of his life, watching over the sheep on the hills, learning to use his sling to protect them whenever wolves or bears drew near. This was his season of preparation. Before he could ever become a shepherd to his people, he had to learn to be a shepherd to his sheep. Before he could ever throw stones at Goliath, he had to throw stones at wolves.

Why did God choose David? The thing about David that God loved was the fact that he had a servant heart right from the beginning. That's rare. It's only been recently that people have taught that leaders should be servants. Robert Greenleaf was in part responsible for this trend. His book *Servant Leadership* took the business world by storm. It cut right across the conventional idea of the leader as a controlling CEO, in a top-down, hierarchical structure. Greenleaf described the most effective leaders as people who serve the people in their organization, as opposed to being served by them. He described leaders as people who empower people in their organization, as opposed to exercising power over them.

Does this sound like anyone you know?

Jesus was the first person in history to teach his followers that leaders are not here to lord it over other people. The authentic leader releases people; he or she does not restrict people. The true leader wields a towel not a sceptre. They wash feet rather than bind peoples' hands. Even Jesus, the King of kings and the Lord of lords, said that he had not come to be served but to serve, and to give his life as a ransom to many (Mark 10:45).

Jesus modelled this! What Greenleaf did was remind the business world what Jesus had taught and embodied in his life. His book is really an extended footnote to what Jesus said and did two thousand years ago.

As so often, the Bible is way ahead of its time and everyone is simply playing catch up with the wisdom of heaven!

The thing we need to remember about Jesus of Nazareth is that he is an exact portrait of what God is really like. If Jesus is the ultimate Servant Leader, then this should tell us something about the Father's heart – that the heart of Almighty God is a self-giving, sacrificial heart.

This, then, is why God adored David. David exhibited the attitude of a servant. In the foundations of his life, David always sought to serve his father in the family business. He sought to serve his family. He even sought to serve his sheep. The attitude of a servant led to the actions of a servant, which is why the Bible describes David as "a man after God's own heart." Even when David

CHAPTER 1 | GETTING ON BOARD

was called to serve a king who had lost his mind and lost his way (King Saul), David still obeyed. What a lesson that is for Christian men!

David therefore built a foundation of service in his life. This was his season of silence, his history of hiddenness, his period of preparation. He did what his father Jesse asked of him; he went out in the daylight and the night hours into the hills to look after the sheep. The Bible describes what happened next, when the prophet Samuel came to Jesse's house to find the future king of Israel:

> *Jesse presented his seven sons to Samuel. Samuel was blunt with Jesse, "GOD hasn't chosen any of these."*
>
> *Then he asked Jesse, "Is this it? Are there no more sons?"*
>
> *"Well, yes, there's the runt. But he's out tending the sheep."*
>
> *Samuel ordered Jesse, "Go get him. We're not moving from this spot until he's here."*
>
> *Jesse sent for him. He was brought in, the very picture of health—bright-eyed, good-looking.*
>
> *GOD said, "Up on your feet! Anoint him! This is the one."*
>
> *Samuel took his flask of oil and anointed him, with his brothers standing around watching. The Spirit of GOD entered David like a rush of wind, God vitally empowering him for the rest of his life.*
>
> (1 Samuel 16, *The Message*)

Did you see what David's father called him? "The runt of the litter." David was the last and the least of Jesse's sons, but it was David whom God had chosen. Why? Because as Samuel said just before this, God looks upon the heart, not upon the outward appearance, and in David's heart he had found someone like Him – someone who delights in serving.

So, don't ever say about yourself, "I'm a *nobody*." God takes hold of the nobodies and turns them into somebodies! He chooses the insignificant and infuses them with significance. He gives extraordinary purposes to ordinary people. He's amazing like that.

This was true of David. When David's opportunity came, he was prepared. He was found ready because he was found serving God in the ordinary and grubby tasks of life.

It can be true of you too.

All you need to do is serve.

Leaving a Legacy

What are people going to say about you when you've gone? What are they going to write on your gravestone or in your obituary? What will your legacy be? What footprint will you leave in the dust of the earth?

There have been many memorable epitaphs written about people after they've died. Here are three of the most inspiring examples of what people have written about the departed on their gravestones:

Beloved father
Bela Lugosi (by his children)

Mother of the Civil Rights Movement
Rosa Parks

A Man of God.
A.W. Tozer.

Here are three more epitaphs, this time humorous:

I told you I was sick
Spike Milligan

Stranger! Approach this spot with gravity,

CHAPTER 1 | GETTING ON BOARD

John Brown is filling his last cavity.
(John Brown was a dentist!)

And, the all-time classic is Benjamin Franklin's epitaph:

The Body of B. Franklin, printer
Like the Cover of an old Book
Its Contents torn out
And stripped of its Lettering & Guilding
Lies here food for worms
For it will, as he believed, appear one more
In a new and more elegant edition
Corrected and Improved by the Author.

These are memorable epitaphs.

One of the most memorable epitaphs in the Bible is the one given to King David. One thousand years after David's death, the Apostle Paul comes up with this unforgettable summary of David's character and life when he is speaking on a sabbath day to fellow Jews in the synagogue in Antioch:

Now, when David had served God's purpose in his generation, he fell asleep.

(Acts 13:36, New International Version)

What an epitaph that is!

In the Bible, falling asleep is used as a picture for the process of dying. It's a hopeful picture because of course our sleeping is followed by an awakening. For the believer, death is but a sleep from which, one day, we shall arise when Jesus comes back to the earth.

Before David fell asleep in death, he did something with his life. *He served God's purpose.* He didn't serve himself because he knew that God's plans were far more important and fulfilling. He discovered what God was doing in his own generation, in his own country and times, and he made it his aim to get behind that with all his might. Instead of asking God to bless David's plans, David decided to bless God's plans instead.

What a man of God!

What an inspiring example!

What a memorable epitaph!

David was presented with the opportunity of a lifetime, and he seized it in the lifetime of that opportunity.

Get in the Galley!

But that's not the half of it! Wait till I tell you what the word "served" really means in the original language of the Book of Acts. When Paul says "served", he uses a very specific Greek word.

HUPERETEO

This is the first-person singular form of the verb.
It means "I serve."

It is made up of two words.

HUPER – meaning "under."

ETEO – meaning "I row."

Paul has in mind here a picture of a galley ship in the Roman navy. This makes sense; Paul's original name was Saul and he grew up in the city of Tarsus in Turkey. This city was part of the Roman Empire and was especially favoured by Rome. As a Jewish man in Tarsus, Saul was given the status of Roman citizen, which meant that he became very familiar with the Roman way of life. Being near an important harbour, it followed that Paul was very aware of the Roman navy. He would frequently have seen biremes (two-decked galleys) and triremes (three-decked galleys) throughout his youth. This was almost certainly in his mind when he gave voice to his epitaph for King David. When he declares that King David *served* (*hupereteo*) God's purpose, the picture is a very powerful one. He is saying that David volunteered to serve in God's fleet and

CHAPTER 1 | GETTING ON BOARD

that he went below decks to work as an oarsman, obeying God's orders.

What a picture that is!

In previous books, I have used the picture of the Roman Army in my attempts to inspire Christian men to fight the good fight and to win the everyday battles we have with the world, the flesh and the devil. You can read about this in books like *Freedom Fighters* and *Behold the Man!* These books take their cue from Paul's call to arms in Ephesians 6, where he compares the Christian life to life as a Roman legionary:

Finally, be strong in the Lord and in his mighty power. Put on the full armour of God, so that you can take your stand against the devil's schemes. For our struggle is not against flesh and blood, but against the rulers, against the authorities, against the powers of this dark world and against the spiritual forces of evil in the heavenly realms. Therefore, put on the full armour of God, so that when the day of evil comes, you may be able to stand your ground, and after you have done everything, to stand. Stand firm then, with the belt of truth buckled around your waist, with the breastplate of righteousness in place, and with your feet fitted with the readiness that comes from the gospel of peace. In addition to all this, take up the shield of faith, with which you can extinguish all the flaming arrows of the evil one. Take the helmet of salvation and the sword of the Spirit, which is the word of God.

In this address, you can clearly see how Paul uses the Roman foot soldier as a picture of what life is like in God's army, in the ongoing struggle between light and darkness that rages in our world. Paul saw Roman legionaries all the time. Using this as an analogy for spiritual warfare came naturally to him.

But Paul wasn't just used to seeing Roman soldiers on land. He also saw them at sea as well, where they performed a role every bit as important as those on *terra firma* in the mighty task of maintaining order in the vast expanses of the Roman Empire in the time of the

New Testament. Without the Roman navies, pirates would have ruled the waves.

You're in the Navy Now

Paul's epitaph for King David is a beautiful summary of one man's life. David volunteered for the Lord's navy, went below decks, and determined to row for his Lord, and fight every battle he was called to fight. David established the *priority* of service early on his life, expressed this through the *practice* of service, and eventually discovered his *purpose* in service.

This is how it will be for us too. We first need to do something with our minds. We need to believe in the value of service and make it a priority in every sphere of our lives. We need to make a mental vow, *I am going to be a servant in every part of my life – home, church, my neighbourhood, workplace, everywhere.*

Then we need to do something with our hands and turn our mental beliefs into practical actions. We need to find ways in which we can express our prioritisation of service in physical ways, remembering what Thomas Edison said, that "Opportunity is missed by most people because it is dressed in overalls and looks like work."

Finally, we need to continue doing this until such time as God shows us what all this has been preparing for – the *purpose* of our lives in this generation. This third stage in the process is a matter of the eyes - the spiritual eyes of our hearts. We all know what our purpose is in general; it is to make disciples of all nations (Matthew 28:18-20). But we also need to know what our specific purpose is. This takes spiritual vision and discernment.

This entire process takes time and it involves our minds, bodies and spirits. In other words, it is an all-encompassing journey, a holistic enterprise in which we collaborate with the Holy Spirit in finding the precise place and task we have in the galley in the Lord's navy.

CHAPTER 1 | GETTING ON BOARD

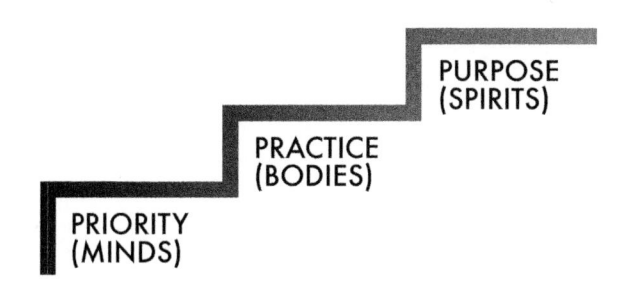

```
                            ┌─── PURPOSE
                            │    (SPIRITS)
                ┌── PRACTICE │
                │   (BODIES) │
   ┌─ PRIORITY  │            │
   │  (MINDS)   │            │
```

All of us want to make our lives count while we have breath in our lungs and strength in our bodies. We all want to leave a productive legacy. But if our lives are to echo in the generation after us, they need to resound in the generation in which we live right now.

Right now, God is looking for men who will get on board his galley ships and become oarsmen in his navy. He is looking for men who will work with him not to bring the whole globe under Roman rule, as in the ancient world, but to bring all the nations into the white-hot glory of His presence. Everything begins with opportunity, with God's *sacred* time invading your *mundane* time.

So, then, will you embrace the opportunity of a lifetime in the lifetime of the opportunity? Will you serve the purposes of God in your generation? Will you get on board?

As you start to read this book, a good thing to do would be to pray the prayer of consecration that John Wesley – the man caught in the storm – prayed. It's often referred to as his "covenant" prayer – a prayer of agreement between him and God. Ask the Holy Spirit to help you with this. Those who really mean these words will surely serve the purpose of God in their generation.

I am no longer my own but yours.
Put me to what you will,
rank me with whom you will;
put me to doing,
put me to suffering;
let me be employed for you,

or laid aside for you,
exalted for you,
or brought low for you;
let me be full,
let me be empty,
let me have all things,
let me have nothing:
I freely and wholeheartedly yield all things
to your pleasure and disposal.
And now, glorious and blessed God,
Father, Son and Holy Spirit,
you are mine and I am yours. So be it.
And the covenant now made on earth, let it be ratified in heaven.

My friends, it's time to get in the galley and row!

> **QUOTE**
>
> There comes a special moment in everyone's life, a moment for which that person was born. That special opportunity, when he seizes it, will fulfil his mission – a mission for which he is uniquely qualified. In that moment, he will find greatness. It is his finest hour.
>
> Winston Churchill

CHAPTER 1 | GETTING ON BOARD

QUESTIONS

1. Am I seizing every small opportunity to serve God?

2. Am I preparing faithfully for my *Kairos* - my big moment of opportunity?

3. Am I maintaining a state of readiness in my ordinary, chronological, mundane time?

4. Am I being faithful to God in my "hidden years"?

5. Am I a man after God's own heart, like David?

6. Am I daily saying YES to God's invitation to get in his galley and row?

7. Am I investing in the legacy that I want to leave for the next generation?

THE 7 VALUES OF THOSE WHO GET IN THE GALLEY AND ROW

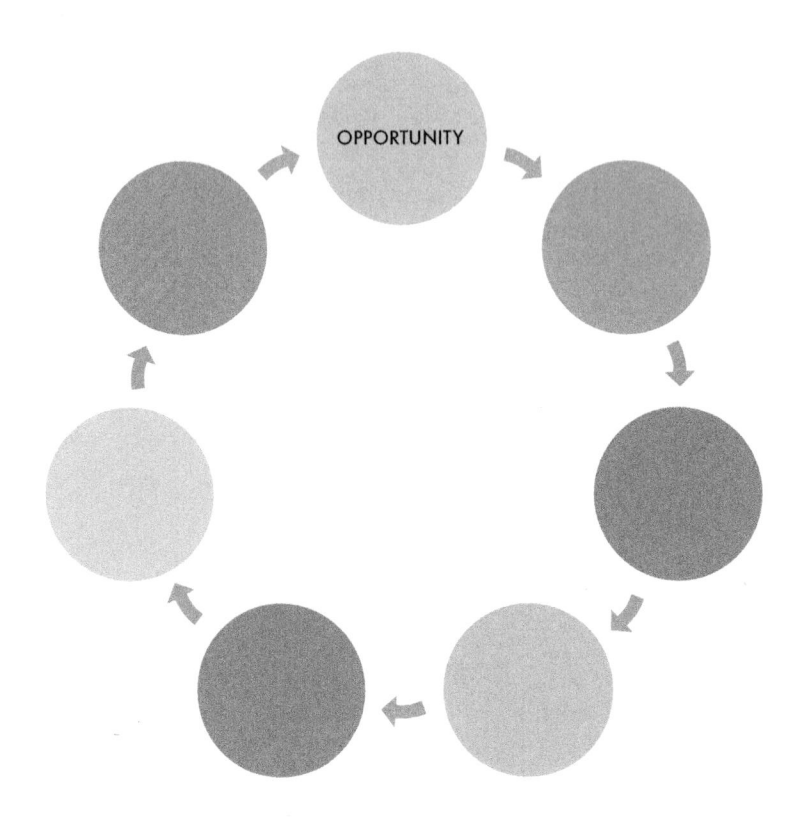

OPPORTUNITY

CHAPTER 2

THE VOLUNTEER SPIRIT

Mel Gibson's movie *Hacksaw Ridge* (2016) is now regarded as one of the greatest war films ever made, gaining six Oscar nominations, winning two, at the 89th Academy Awards. As a biographical drama, it celebrates, in sometimes brutal and graphic ways, the heroic service of a man called Private Desmond Doss who was awarded the Medal of Honour for his exceptional courage.

After the Japanese attack on Pearl Harbour in December 1941, Doss's neighbours and friends back in his hometown are desperate to volunteer to serve in the US Army. Some are accepted and go off to fight. Others are refused on medical and other grounds. Some of these are so devastated by the refusal that they take their lives.

Doss (played brilliantly by Andrew Garfield) is also filled with a passion to serve. However, he is a devout Christian man who takes the Ten Commandments very seriously. He cannot therefore in good conscience sign up to fight. He is a pacifist and a conscientious objector. He therefore decides to volunteer to serve as an army combat medic. Doing this, he can fulfil his passion to serve and at the same time stay true to his Christian convictions. His dilemma is therefore supposedly solved.

Except that it isn't.

When Doss volunteers, he is faced with one test after another. There is firstly his relationship with his father. Tom Desmond (Hugo Weaving) is traumatised because of his experiences in

WW1. He lost some of his friends at the Front; these men had also volunteered. In a futile effort to blot out the memories, Tom has become an alcoholic.

In one poignant scene, Tom takes Desmond to see their graves and tells him that he's going to become just like them. Desmond, however, sticks to his principles and tells his father that he is going to go and serve, whatever his father says or does. "While everybody else is taking life, I'm going to be saving it," he tells him. "That's going to be my way to serve."

Doss pushes past this first obstacle but then finds a second, far bigger, problem. When he starts his training, he refuses to pick up a rifle when ordered to do so by his drill sergeant (acted by Vince Vaughn). Private Doss has already decided that he's not going to carry a weapon, let alone fire one.

This lands Doss in a world of grief. He is summoned to an army court to explain his actions. There is every chance that he is going to be sent to prison for disobeying orders. His fiancée Dorothy is desperately worried. When she visits him in his holding cell, he tells her that he cannot dilute his principles and carry a rifle into battle. He says, "I don't know how I'm going to live with myself if I don't stay true to what I believe."

When his trial begins, the judge asks Doss what's driving him to serve in the Army if he's not prepared to take up arms. "Why is it so important to you," he asks, "given your refusal to even touch a weapon to serve in a combat unit?" Doss's reply is worth quoting in full.

"Because when the Japanese attacked Pearl Harbour, I took it personal. Everyone I knew was on fire to join up, including me. There were two men in my hometown declared 4-F unfit. They killed themselves because they couldn't serve. Why, I had a job in a defence plant, and I could've taken a deferment, but that ain't right. It isn't right that other men should fight and die, that I would just be sitting at home safe. I need to serve. I got the energy and the passion to serve as a medic, right in the middle with the other guys. No less danger, just…while everybody else is taking life, I'm going to be saving it."

Did you notice the number of times Doss uses the word "serve" in that speech? I can count three times. I've put them in italics.

Doss' concluding remark is memorable.

"With the world so set on tearing itself apart, it doesn't seem like such a bad thing to me to wanna put a little bit of it back together."

In the end, it is the appearance of Doss's father – in his Great War uniform – that helps to persuade the court. He pleads on behalf of his son to the Brigadier General in charge of the court proceedings. This saves the day and Doss is sent off to the Pacific to be part of the invasion force at Okinawa, the location for one of WW2's most horrific battles. There he saves wounded men who are lying in the middle of hell, waiting for enemy soldiers to shoot or bayonet them. It is a task fraught with unimaginable perils, but Doss relies on God, drawing his strength from his faith, and his prayer is simply this: "Please Lord, help me get one more. Help me get one more."

The Ben-Hur Fallacy

In the 2001 film *Pearl Harbour*, Colonel Jimmy Doolittle (Alec Baldwin) decides to lead a daring bombing raid on Tokyo in retaliation for the Japanese surprise attack on Pearl Harbour. He asks men to volunteer for this mission, telling them that it is certain that most of them will not make it home; there won't be enough fuel to get back and those that do survive the bombing run will have to crash land in China. However, all the men volunteer for the mission and engage in a three-month spell of intensive training. Just before they set off to attack Tokyo, Doolittle says, "There's nothing stronger than the heart of a volunteer."

What both Doolittle and Doss have in common is what is often referred to as the "volunteer spirit." No man of God can ever fulfil God's plan for their lives without having this willingness to serve. Remember what I said about Acts 13:38 in the last chapter? The Apostle Paul, delivering the finest epitaph for King David's life, said that David *served* the purpose of God in his own generation. I pointed out that the word translated "serve" in the original language refers to going below decks in a galley and then performing the duties of an oarsmen. Paul took this picture from the world of the Roman navy. He was thinking of the Roman galleys, describing David as one of God's "under rowers."

What picture do you have, if any, of these oarsmen?

I suspect, if you're of a certain age, your image will have been greatly influenced by yet another famous movie, *Ben-Hur* (1959). Judah Ben-Hur (played by Charlton Heston) is a wealthy Jewish prince and merchant in Jerusalem in AD 26, a few years before the crucifixion of Christ. During a parade for the new governor of Judea called Gratus, some loose tiles fall from Judah Ben-Hur's house. When they smash on the ground, the new governor's horse is spooked and Gratus himself is nearly killed. Furious, Ben-Hur's childhood friend, Messala (the Roman governor of the Antonia Fortress) condemns Ben-Hur to become a galley slave. Judah swears revenge on his ex-friend Messala as he is led away with all the other prisoners in a long march to the ships.

On the way, stopping in Nazareth, Judah and his fellow victims stop to water the horses of the Roman legionaries. Judah is desperately thirsty and begs his Roman captors for a drink. They refuse and he collapses. A stranger passing by stoops to help him. He offers him a drink. Who is this benefactor? We learn that it is none other than Jesus of Nazareth. Ben-Hur never forgets this encounter over the next three years as a galley slave.

It's a compelling story, isn't it?

Except that it's based on a falsehood.

It's founded entirely on the idea that in the time of Jesus the galleys were made up of people who were *forced* to row for the Roman Empire. This fiction has informed the popular imagination ever since. Our idea of Roman oarsmen is dictated by the picture of Charlton Heston in chains, wearing only a loin cloth, his torso covered in sweat, pulling his oar to the relentless beat of a drum. It is a picture of slavery, of men forced against their will to do something as a punishment for a crime.

Historians now tell us that this is not a true reflection of the facts. Those who became oarsmen were not galley slaves; they were volunteers. Most often, they were men who had volunteered for the Roman Army, trained as soldiers, but who decided that they wanted to serve as part of Caesar's navy, at sea, not on land. The Roman galleys were therefore manned by freemen not slaves. Those who served in them were not pressganged into maritime slavery. They chose this life as an act of their own free will. Only in the rarest and most extreme circumstances was a person compelled to become a galley slave, but this was the exception to the rule. The rule was that men signed up for this life.

In short, oarsmen exhibited the volunteer spirit.

They possessed the courage to serve.

The Greatest Virtue

Courage, as we saw in *Behold the Man* was one of the greatest virtues in the Roman world in the time of the New Testament. The word "virtue" has "vir" at the front, a word that in Latin means "man." It is the word from which we get *virile* and *virility*. In Roman culture, men were called to be virtuous and the virtues they were supposed to embody were the qualities of the "manly man." Courage, or fortitude, was an essential quality for a man in the Roman Empire. In fact, it was held to be the most important manly quality of all, the highest of all the virtues, the one on which all the other virtues depended. Become a courageous man, and all the other virtues would fall into place.

When the Apostle Paul tells us that "David served the purpose of God in his generation," he is not saying that God, or someone else like the Prophet Samuel, forced David to serve. He is saying that David volunteered as an under rower in God's navy. David chose of his own free will to sign up to serve God in his own life and times. It was something he wanted to do. It was what burned in his heart, which is why God expresses such affection for David in the Scriptures. David was a man after God's own heart. Why? Because God has, for all eternity, chosen of his own sovereign and free will to serve humanity, first by creating the world, second by redeeming it.

Our God is truly the Servant King.

Just as David was.

And being a volunteer requires immense bravery. Desmond Doss shows us that. Colonel Doolittle demonstrates it too. From the moment they signed up for their missions, they were faced with one test after another. Meeting these tests head on, overcoming them in turn, required courage.

Brené Brown says this: "you can choose courage and you can choose comfort, but you cannot choose both." Those men who volunteer to serve God, whether as an army combat medic or as an Old Testament Warrior King, are men who choose courage over comfort. They are men who freely decide to break out of their comfort zones, to face immense difficulties, in order to serve God's purpose in their generation.

And here's the thing.

The tests come early.

Very early.

Right at the beginning, in fact.

Think of Desmond Doss. No sooner has he decided to sign up than he is tested and taunted by his own father. No sooner has he started training, than his own sergeant is on his back for not picking up a rifle. The next moment he has a gigantic challenge on his hand – persuading a military tribunal that he must be allowed to be a medic who does not carry or use arms in battle.

King David was no different.

In 1 Samuel 16, he is anointed by the prophet Samuel. Out of all the sons of Hesse, it is David – "the runt of the litter" – who is the man born to be king. When Samuel anoints him, David is filled with the Holy Spirit. He is anointed for active service.

The Oil and the Toil

You'd think that was it.

David is anointed.

But straight after 1 Samuel 16 comes 1 Samuel 17.

No great revelation there.

But what's in 1 Samuel 17?

The story of David and Goliath.

And Goliath is a gigantic challenge – literally.

As with Private Doss, and indeed every other man of God who has the courage to volunteer, the blessing is followed immediately by a battle. The fullness is followed by the fight.

Think of Ephesians chapters 5 and 6. In Ephesians 5, Paul tells us to go on being filled with the Holy Spirit. That's *fullness*. That's the anointing. That's the oil. In the very next chapter, he is telling us to put on the whole armour of God and, like a good soldier, to stand with other men of God against the devil's schemes. That's the *fight*. That's toil. It's blood, sweat, and tears.

This divine pattern is visible in the lives of all the great men of God, pre-eminently Jesus himself. In the River Jordan, he is filled with the Holy Spirit in a glorious and lavish demonstration of the

Father's love. That's *fullness* again. But what happens next? He is told to go out into the desert to faceoff with the devil. There's the *fight* again. After the oil, comes the toil.

Being anointed doesn't inoculate you against discomfort. Far from it. Being filled with the Spirit is the prelude to facing great fights. Without the help of the Holy Spirit, you'd never make it through the battlefield to the place of victory. Without the power of God, you'd never meet the challenges head on and conquer them. With God's help, and only with his help, you get to turn your test into a testimony. You get to tell your own stories of slaying giants. That's why it takes immense bravery to volunteer to serve.

Look at David's first test. This is The Message version of the story of Goliath in 1 Samuel 17:

A giant nearly ten feet tall stepped out from the Philistine line into the open, Goliath from Gath. He had a bronze helmet on his head and was dressed in armour - 126 pounds of it! He wore bronze shin guards and carried a bronze sword. His spear was like a fence rail - the spear tip alone weighed over fifteen pounds. His shield bearer walked ahead of him.

At this stage, David is not at the scene. This is a description of what Goliath has been doing, appearing in front of the Israelite army, taunting them for their lack of courage, calling on someone to fight him.

Goliath stood there and called out to the Israelite troops, "Why bother using your whole army? Am I not Philistine enough for you? And you're all committed to Saul, aren't you? So pick your best fighter and pit him against me. If he gets the upper hand and kills me, the Philistines will all become your slaves. But if I get the upper hand and kill him, you'll all become our slaves and serve us. I challenge the troops of Israel this day. Give me a man. Let us fight it out together!"

No one volunteers to fight Goliath. King Saul, and all his soldiers, are petrified. But then, as the cliché goes, "cometh the

CHAPTER 2 | THE VOLUNTEER SPIRIT

hour, cometh the man." The boy who has just been anointed by the prophet Samuel arrives on the scene, and his reaction is altogether different.

Enter David.

He was the son of Jesse the Ephrathite from Bethlehem in Judah. Jesse, the father of eight sons, was himself too old to join Saul's army. Jesse's three oldest sons had followed Saul to war. The names of the three sons who had joined up with Saul were Eliab, the firstborn; next, Abinadab; and third, Shammah. David was the youngest son. While his three oldest brothers went to war with Saul, David went back and forth from attending to Saul to tending his father's sheep in Bethlehem.

David watches Goliath posturing and mocking for forty days. No one rises to meet the challenge. Not even his own older brothers, part of Saul's army. In fact, when David's dad sends him to the front lines to check in on his brothers, they round on him, criticizing him for coming to spectate on the battle. How often the greatest tests to our calling come from within our own homes and families. This was true of Desmond Doss. This was true of David.

But David is not a spectator; he's a servant. He's one who has already started to serve God's purposes in his own day. He has received the oil in 1 Samuel 16. He is about to accept the toil in 1 Samuel 17.

When King Saul hears what David's brothers have been saying, he calls for him. This is the opportunity David needs; he is in front of the King and in pole position to volunteer. What does David say?

"Master," said David, "don't give up hope. I'm ready to go and fight this Philistine."

In other words, "Let me at him!"

That's the courage of the volunteer, right there.

Five Smooth Stones

When King Saul tells David that he's too young and inexperienced, David retorts that he has been preparing all his life for this moment. He's been a shepherd boy out on the hills, protecting his father's flocks of sheep. Whenever predators tried to steal and eat the sheep, he aimed his sling and fired a stone at them, killing them instantly. "I've had years of practice," David is saying. "If I can kill a bear or a lion, I can kill this ugly blot on Israel's honour."

Saul relents and David heads for a nearby brook, where he chooses five smooth stones. There have been many interpretations why David chooses five stones. Some say this the four extra stones are David's backup plan. But I think that's wrong. We know from 2 Samuel 21:15-22 that Goliath had four brothers, all just as big, hairy and ungodly as he was. Three of their names are given in that passage: Ishbi-benob, Saph, and another man called Goliath. The fourth isn't named but is said to have six fingers on both his hands, six toes on both feet. They sound very friendly, don't they?!

Here's the real reason why David takes five stones.

He's not just after Goliath.

He wants to finish Goliath's brothers too.

He's not just after one giant; he's after the lot!

And in 1 Samuel 22:22, we learn that he killed them all.

Starting with Goliath.

When Goliath taunts David for being so small and defenceless, David replies that he doesn't come with weapons and armour but with his faith in the name of Almighty God, the Lord of the Armies of Heaven.

Let's pause a moment here.

What's David doing? He's making a conscious choice to prefer

CHAPTER 2 | THE VOLUNTEER SPIRIT

faith over fear. Faith and fear are two ends of the same spectrum. Fear says, "I believe that something negative is about to happen in my life." Faith says, "I believe something positive is about to happen in my life." Fear gives into the darkness; faith surrenders to the light. Fear says, "Goliath is so big, he's going to crush me." Faith says, "Goliath is so big I can't miss!"

Faith believes that what is not yet seen will be seen, and what will be seen will be good. When a man of God chooses faith, he chooses to say, "I believe it, therefore I'll see it, and when I see it, it's going to be good. Really good."

This is the exact opposite of the way the world thinks.

Worldly people say, "I'll believe it when I see it."

The man of God says, "I'll see it when I believe it."

Listen to what David says to Goliath. It is the perfect articulation of faith. It is the undiluted, uncompromising expression of a certain hope. He says, "I'm about to kill you, cut off your head, and serve up your body and the bodies of your Philistine buddies to the crows and coyotes. The whole earth will know that there's an extraordinary God in Israel. And everyone gathered here will learn that GOD doesn't save by means of sword or spear. The battle belongs to GOD—he's handing you to us on a platter!"

And that's exactly what happens.

Down in the Valley of Elah, David uses his sling and aims a stone at Goliath's head. The stone penetrates the giant's skull. The huge enemy falls to the ground with a mighty thump, causing clouds of dust to waft into the air. There is a gasp from everyone, both the Israelite and the Philistine soldiers. David, meanwhile, runs to the giant's corpse and lops off his enemy's head with the giant's own sword. Why? David only had a sling and five stones. He didn't even bring a blade to the battle!

And seeing their champion defeated and dead, the enemy troops run for their lives, scattering in all directions.

David has passed the test.

He has showed great courage in volunteering and extraordinary bravery in the battle. He has used the first his five smooth stones. There are four still left. They're for Goliath's brothers.

Fourteen Types of Test

Why does it take courage for a man to do what David did and to serve God's purpose in their generation? Why does it require bravery to go down below decks and row for Jesus in the bowels of the galley?

The truth is, the moment a person says "yes" to the call to serve, they are going to be tested. If you don't want to face tests and trials, if you just want a comfortable Christian life, then don't obey the call to get in the galley and row. Don't set your heart on serving God's purpose. Just serve your own purpose. Choose to be self-oriented rather than God-oriented. Devise your own plan for your life and live a life of comfort and ease. Don't, whatever you do, decide to become an under rower in God's galley ships. Don't do it. You'll have to leave your comfort zone. You'll have to choose courage.

In his book, *The Making of a Leader*, Frank Damazio identifies fourteen different tests that leaders face in the Bible. No one leader faces all fourteen, but the chances are, if you're like Private Doss or King David, you're going to face at least some of these. The definitions of each test are my own descriptions, although they are loosely linked to Damazio's.

Time Test

This is when God has spoken to you about what he wants to do in your life, but he seems to be taking an awfully long time activating it. The time test is when we are tempted to give up in the time lag between the revelation and its appointed time. This test is designed to develop the stature of waiting in us.

CHAPTER 2 | THE VOLUNTEER SPIRIT

Word Test

This is when God gives us a word about our calling, and we need to grow in our understanding of what this means. It's the glory of God to conceal a matter, so sometimes it's not easy to understand the word. We need to move from revelation to interpretation and then from interpretation to application.

Character Test

This is exactly how it sounds. God tests the mettle of our character by permitting us to be exposed to a context full of temptations (particularly, money, sex and power). If we compromise, we can delay, disrupt or destroy our unique call to serve his purpose in our generation.

Motivation Test

This is similar. God allows circumstances to develop in our lives that reveal the true intentions of our hearts and the real reasons why we want to serve him. These circumstances will unveil the secrets of our hearts – such as the motivation to make money out of ministry, or to have a platform in ministry.

Servant Test

Submission is the higher law. God tests the authenticity of our will-to-serve by putting us in places where we must serve another man's ministry with complete fidelity and loyalty. Only when we have learned to be hardworking and trustworthy in the second chair will he allow us to sit and serve in the first chair!

Wilderness Test

Remember Moses? He had to serve for forty years in the back side of the desert – as dry and barren season indeed. Only after he had been faithful in the smaller task of looking after his father-in-law's sheep was he released into the bigger destiny of delivering his own people from slavery.

Misunderstanding Test

Remember Joseph? Joseph had a dream. That's what the Bible tells us. But his own brothers misunderstood what the dream signified and resented him for it. When others, particularly family members, misunderstand what God has called us to do, that's a big test. David experienced this too.

Patience Test

Patience comes from a Latin word (*patiens*) meaning "suffering." The patience test is any kind of suffering that we need to endure in order to fulfil our calling to serve God's purpose for our generation. Any test that makes us think of giving up, that questions whether we will go through with this, is a patience test.

Frustration Test

For much of a large part of a man of God's life, he may be called to experience a lack of alignment or convergence between his passion and profession. Waiting for these two things to line up can lead to frustration, but if we pass the frustration test, we will graduate to true fulfilment.

Discouragement Test

Elijah went through a season of discouragement, even depression, and so do most men of God, if they're real and honest. It can be hard to rejoice when there's no fruit in our ministry, or no fulfilment in our work. Passing the discouragement test is dependent on men of God sharing honestly with each other in these times.

Warfare Test

No man of God is going to have a battle-free life. All of us face intense opposition. Some of this comes in the form of direct demonic assault. Some indirectly through obstructive people or situations. We all need to put on the armour of God and use our authority in Christ in such times.

Self-Will Test

This is a test in which what I want and what God wills come into conflict. I may want to do things my way, but if God is saying do it differently, or don't do it all, I complain. When it's my way or the High Way, always choose the High Way. It may be harder in the short term, but far less costly in the long run.

Vision Test

Sometimes we only see very little of God's purposes for our lives. We see in part, not in full. At these times it's tough to keep on trusting God, obeying what little of the vision he's given for us to see today. We want it all, and we want it now. But sometimes he tests us by showing us a little rather than a lot.

Usage Test

These are the times when we feel left on the shelf, when we feel our gifts aren't being recognized or used, when we feel unappreciated and unused in God's service. React in the flesh, and we may miss our destiny. Respond in the Spirit, and it's only a matter of time before we seize it.

The Courage to Serve

God is looking for men like David who are brave enough to put their hands up and say, "Here I am, Lord. I'll volunteer." David made serving God a priority and then a practice. Eventually, it became his purpose. David had the strongest heart of all, the heart of a volunteer. These are the kinds of men that God is looking for today. Men who will leave their comfort zones and face every test head on; men who will be ready to do anything for God and will say with Isaiah the prophet, "Here I am, Lord. Send me."

In 2 Chronicles 16:9 we read that "the eyes of the LORD move to and fro throughout the earth that He may strongly support those whose heart is completely His."

God promises to support strongly the heart that is sold out for him. In other words, if you choose to serve him, he will choose to support you. You won't be going alone. You won't be doing this on your own.

Will you volunteer to serve?

Will you get in the galley and row?

Will you choose courage over comfort?

Winston Churchill said this: "Courage is rightly esteemed the first of human qualities because it has been said, it is the quality which guarantees all others." Let's prove that by hearing and obeying God's word to Joshua.

"Haven't I commanded you? Strength! Courage! Don't be timid; don't get discouraged. GOD, your God, is with you every step you take."

Joshua 1:9

You hear that? EVERY step you take.

My friends, it's time to get in the galley and row!

> **QUOTE**
> *If service is beneath you, then leadership is beyond you.*
> **Nicky Gumbel**

CHAPTER 2 | THE VOLUNTEER SPIRIT

QUESTIONS

1. Do you have "the heart of a volunteer?"?

2. Are you willingly rowing in God's galley today?

3. Which are you choosing in your life – courage or comfort?

4. Are you a spectator or a servant?

5. What Goliaths are you called to confront?

6. Which of the fourteen leadership tests have you faced so far?

7. Is your heart wholly His?

THE 7 VALUES OF THOSE WHO GET IN THE GALLEY AND ROW

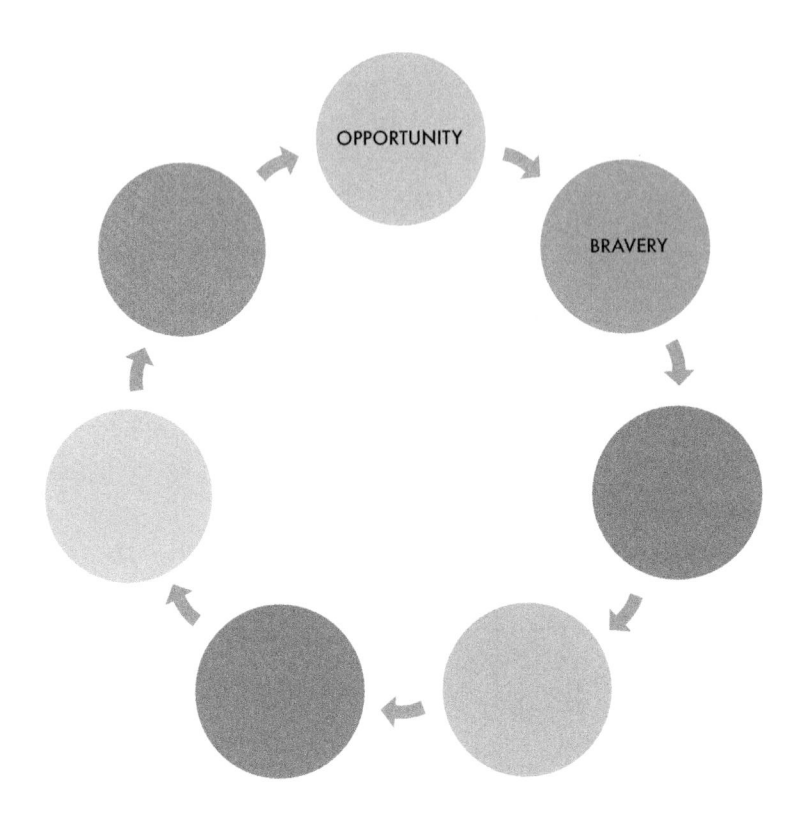

- OPPORTUNITY
- BRAVERY

CHAPTER 3

MEN UNDER AUTHORITY

I have a very good friend who had a long and effective ministry as a pastor. He served as an associate pastor in two churches before going on to lead two more. The fourth and final church that he led grew in revival to over 1700 members. People from all over the world came to visit it to learn the hallmarks of success. That church, and the pastor who led it, were lauded by many. It was one of the largest and fastest growing churches in the UK at the time.

If you asked my friend the secrets of leading prosperously from the first chair, he would answer that it was by first learning to serve patiently in the second chair. The truth is, none of the highs he experienced in the fourth church would ever have been possible without the lows he experienced in his first church. He worked there for four years in very trying circumstances. At home, his wife suffered from post-natal depression during the whole of his time there, and his first child cried incessantly, suffering from a severe case of cholic. At church, he served under a very controlling senior pastor who demanded that he work twelve-hour days six days a week, leaving him little room for recharging his batteries, let alone serving his wife and child.

What was the problem here?

The senior pastor concerned had been in the navy and expected everyone under his ministry to behave like people of a junior rank. This extended not only to my friend and to all the other members of the staff team. It also extended to the church members. As much as people tried to like and even love him, everyone ended up exhausted by him. This went for those outside the church too. Funeral directors and others were all expected to fall in line and obey orders. Everyone was supposed to do what they were told.

Today, we would call this "spiritual abuse", but back in the early and mid-1980s, we really had no such terminology for this kind of toxic leadership style. My friend just had to knuckle down and somehow endure the experience. He was a resilient man, but this stretched him to the limits of his patience. Every day, both at home and at work, was fraught with tests.

In the end, there was a lightbulb moment that helped him to keep on running and serving well. A Ugandan pastor visited the church – a man who loved the Bible and was full of the Spirit. He discerned very quickly what was going on in the relationship between my friend and his boss. He therefore took my friend on one side and spoke to him.

"I have seen what you're going through," he said.

My friend was moved by that. Up until then, he had felt alone, and his sense of isolation had only added to his feeling of oppression.

"I believe I have a word from the Lord to encourage you," he added.

My friend was all ears; it had been a long time since anyone had given him anything that had strengthened his heart.

"The years you spend here are intended by God to grow the fruit of the Spirit in you. The years you spend in your next church, wherever that is, are intended by God to grow the gifts of the Spirit in you."

What a wonderful word! Perhaps it won't surprise you to learn that today that man is the Archbishop of Uganda!

And that's exactly what happened to my friend. Over the four years that he served faithfully and patiently under a very difficult man, the Holy Spirit worked in him to cultivate the nine qualities associated with the fruit of the Spirit in Galatians 5: love, joy, peace, patience, kindness, goodness, faithfulness, gentleness and self-control. If he hadn't felt the pressure of these adverse circumstances, my friend would never have been able to grow in these virtues.

But then, after four years, he finished well, left the church, and God moved him on to a new church in a different city.

This new church was one in which the supernatural gifts of the Holy Spirit were welcomed. My friend's new senior pastor and boss was a much healthier man, a man who loved the Word (the Bible) and the power of God's Spirit. Consequently, just as the prophecy had said, my friend grew in the gifts of the Spirit, the nine listed in 1 Corinthians 12: the supernatural word of knowledge, anointed wisdom, special faith, gifts of healing, miracles, prophecy, discernment, speaking in tongues and interpretation of tongues.

After four years of sitting in the second chair in this new church, he had begun to cultivate both the fruit and the gifts of the Spirit, just as God had purposed and promised through a mighty man of God.

A Man Under Authority

In this book we're unpacking Acts 13:38 where Paul says of King David that he served God's purpose in his generation. This is a great epitaph, one that's going to take the whole of this book to understand. As I've already shown, the word "served" contains a picture taken from the Roman navy in the time of the New Testament, the time of the Roman Empire. This navy was made up of galleys that had two, three, four and even sometimes five decks. When Paul says that David served God, he pictures David volunteering to serve below decks in one of these galleys. David, in other words, became an oarsman in God's navy. He obeyed orders by rowing when he was told to row, listening to the beat of the drum below decks, timing his strokes with their unrelenting rhythm.

When Paul used the word "served" of David, he implied that David had at least one abiding quality in his spiritual character. That quality was a virtue called *humility*. It took humility for David to see himself as a servant. He was, after all, destined to become the greatest earthly king in Israel's history. To any lesser man, this sense of destiny would have made him proud. The activation of this destiny when he took the throne could have gone to his head.

But it didn't.

Why?

God had taken David on a journey in which his pride was dealt a death blow and in which his humility would be cultivated over a long period of time. That journey required him to serve for many years as a man under authority. This involved, firstly, being under his father Jesse's authority. David was given the job of being the shepherd boy. He could have complained about that, but he didn't. His older brothers were given more prestigious and fulfilling roles, but David didn't moan. He simply got on with what his father had asked him to do, learning in the process to be a man under authority.

Secondly, it involved working directly for King Saul. Now here's where it gets a whole lot more difficult. If David thought that his season serving his dad's sheep had been trying, that was nothing compared to working under Saul. In fact, no sooner had David been anointed by Samuel, no sooner had David been filled with the Holy Spirit and empowered for service, than he found himself exposed to Saul's unhealthy personality.

The Bible says in 1 Samuel 16 that a black mood of depression descended upon King Saul as soon as David was anointed by Samuel. This depression tormented Saul and made him utterly miserable. The only thing that alleviated this dark mood, lifting it momentarily from Saul's mind, was music.

Now at this point it's worth noting that not only had David been watching his sheep on the hills, he'd also learned how to play the lyre and had become both an accomplished musician and songwriter.

CHAPTER 3 | MEN UNDER AUTHORITY

Out on the hills, he had learned how to sing, and he had learned how to sling!

See again how God works in our hidden seasons of preparation. When preparation meets opportunity, he knows what we are going to need in order to seize the opportunity of a lifetime in the lifetime of that opportunity. David would need to know how to sing as well as sling!

And the first thing he does, before using his sling, is sing.

Jesse took a donkey, loaded it with a couple of loaves of bread, a flask of wine, and a young goat, and sent his son David with it to Saul. David came to Saul and stood before him. Saul liked him immediately and made him his right-hand man. Saul sent word back to Jesse: "Thank you. David will stay here. He's just the one I was looking for. I'm very impressed by him."

After that, whenever the bad depression from God tormented Saul, David got out his harp and played. That would calm Saul down, and he would feel better as the moodiness lifted.

We can only imagine what this must have been like for David in practice. At any time of the day or night, he could have been summoned by Saul to sing him into a place of peace. There were no CD players or Smart Phones with music apps that David could simply switch on and leave with Saul. David had to play live over Saul, soothing him back to sleep in the middle of the night, playing melodies that brought Saul a sense of respite in the middle of the day. That was costly for David, but it was a vital part of learning to serve below decks, rowing to the beat of another man's drum, sailing on a course that another man had determined, whatever the time of day or night.

That's what it means to be a man under authority.

The King's Armour

Saul, not surprisingly, is very impressed by David and appoints him to be his right-hand man. Today, we would call this "sitting in the second chair." Saul sits in the first chair (the throne). David sits in the second chair as his assistant. Saul is the senior leader. David is his associate.

This must have been both frustrating and confusing at times for the young David. After all, the prophet Samuel had anointed him and, as far as he must have been concerned, his elevation to the first chair must have seemed only a smooth pebble's throw away. But it wasn't. We might put it this way. David had the anointing but not the position. Saul had the position but not the anointing. If you don't believe me, read 1 Samuel 16:14: "At that very moment, the Spirit of God left Saul." What moment was that? The moment that David was anointed by Samuel to be king over all Israel.

It goes without saying here that what God wanted for David was a season of what we might call CD Time. CD stands for Character Development. David had things to learn in the gap between receiving the anointing for kingship and assuming the position of king. This is how our loving Heavenly Father often works in our lives. Before he does a great work *through* us, he must first do a great work in us. That inner maturing process is vital, and it takes greater and greater amounts of humility to graduate to higher and higher levels of maturity. If we are prepared to go low, God will let us go high. As St Augustine once said,

"Do you wish to rise? Begin by descending. You plan a tower that will pierce the clouds? Lay first the foundation of humility."

In his book, *Leading from the Second Chair*, Mark Bonem rightly points out, "Too many leaders focus all their energy on moving to the next chair as quickly as possible, and they miss the opportunity to develop their gifts in the current chair." This is a mistake. David had to learn to submit for a season to King Saul's authority. He had to learn to make the most of his time of preparation in the second chair, even though at times this was restrictive rather than releasing, frustrating rather than fulfilling.

There's a lot we could say here about David's CD Time but

CHAPTER 3 | MEN UNDER AUTHORITY

perhaps the standout episode is the earliest of the tests he faces while learning to be accountable to a driven, insecure and demanding leader. This occurs in the story of David's defeat of Goliath. Just before going out to face his giant, Saul tries to force David to wear his armour.

Then Saul gave David his own armour—a bronze helmet and a coat of mail. David put it on, strapped the sword over it, and took a step or two to see what it was like, for he had never worn such things before.

"I can't go in these," he protested to Saul. "I'm not used to them." So, David took them off again.

This is a curious moment in the story. What's going on here? A positive reading of this would claim that Saul is looking out for David, trying to give him as much protection as possible in the face of monumental odds. Good leaders do this; they protect the backs of those that serve under them. But Saul is not a good leader; he is a toxic leader. He is so insecure and unhealed in his heart that he figures that if David wears his armour and wins, everyone will think that the king has vanquished the giant, not the shepherd boy.

Saul's behaviour here is typical of the kind of thing we see even today, especially in the lives of emotionally unhealthy leaders.

Emotionally unhealthy leaders want you to look like them, sound like them, walk like them and even dress like them. This is because they are deep down insecure and afraid.

Emotionally unhealthy leaders claim to be watching over you and fighting for your best interests when they are only interested in their own interests and in feathering their own nest.

Emotionally unhealthy leaders get you to do the dirty and the dangerous work while they sit back and enjoy the benefits of their position. Like Saul, they rest in the tent while you toil on the battlefield.

Emotionally unhealthy leaders take all the credit for what you've done, leaving you to feel undervalued, unappreciated, disillusioned and thoroughly exploited by the whole process.

Why, then, did David have to go through all this? Why didn't God just remove Saul and instate David? It's because serving Saul was necessary for David's development of character. What Saul was doing was projecting his own sense of shame on his younger protégé. Saul should have gone to God for healing for that sense of shame but chose demonic counterfeits to that healing journey, making David's life very challenging. But David never lost his respect for Saul's position, nor his patience in waiting for his own time. He was humble enough to sit in the second chair and gracious enough to work as an oarsman before being promoted to the role of steersman.

How to Make Jesus Happy

There's a story in the Gospels about a Roman centurion. Matthew tells this story in chapter 8 of his Gospel. At the start of the episode, the Roman centurion approaches Jesus with a request.

When Jesus had entered Capernaum, a centurion came to him, asking for help. "Lord," he said, "my servant lies at home paralyzed, suffering terribly."

We can already see something remarkable about this centurion, even in these words. He's a man who really looks after those who serve him. He's a person who cares properly and practically for those working under him. This is genuine compassion and it is emotionally healthy leadership. It is leadership that goes the extra mile for others in the team. In fact, this soldier is so concerned about his servant that he takes the trouble to find Jesus in Capernaum, a town in Galilee where Jesus was making a name for himself healing many sick people from all kinds of conditions and diseases. That is remarkable in itself; Roman centurions were deeply suspicious about popular Jewish men like Jesus. They could be troublemakers, Rome-haters, insurrectionists even. This army officer was taking a

CHAPTER 3 | MEN UNDER AUTHORITY

huge risk. He was clearly desperate to see his servant healed. That's how much the man cared.

Here's Jesus' response.

Jesus said to him, "Shall I come and heal him?"

Jesus responds by asking a question. Is he unsure about the correct procedure here? Is he buying time? None of the above. He is waiting to see something of the Roman centurion's character.

The centurion replied, "Lord, I do not deserve to have you come under my roof. But just say the word, and my servant will be healed. For I myself am a man under authority, with soldiers under me. I tell this one, 'Go,' and he goes; and that one, 'Come,' and he comes. I say to my servant, 'Do this,' and he does it".

Jesus is delighted by these remarks. He loves the character of this soldier. There is something so attractive about this man's inner personality, that Jesus acts straightaway. He doesn't go to the servant's bed and heal him with the power of his touch. He issues a command, a decree, a word of authority, stating that the man is healed at that very moment.

When Jesus heard this, he was amazed and said to those following him, "Truly I tell you, I have not found anyone in Israel with such great faith."

Here is a man who made Jesus very happy.

How?

By showing that he had the humility to be a man under authority. This Roman officer knew about the chain of command. He was a military man, after all. He knew that when his commanding officer gave him an order, his duty was to obey the word and carry it out to the letter. Similarly, when he himself told someone what to do, he expected him to do the same, to reveal their humility by exercising their accountability. Accountability is the twin virtue of humility. The humble man is an accountable man.

Do you want to make Jesus happy?

Then sit in the second chair for a season, grow in humility, and learn to practice accountability. By this you show what Jesus calls "faith." Faith could be translated "faithfulness." It means exercising fidelity under pressure. It means utter dependence on God during the tough seasons. It means knowing your place in God's scheme of things during this period of your life and accepting this cheerfully. It means holding onto the promises of God, the things that he's spoken to you about your destiny, even when they seem furthest from being fulfilled. It above all means never ever giving up, quitting, or compromising. It means staying true and staying the course, following Jesus until he releases you into an acceleration of your purpose and a graduation in your authority.

Put your Hands to the Oar

Even at this early stage in his journey, David was tomorrow's man while Saul had become yesterday's man. How hard it is to serve in the bowels of a galley, knowing that you are called to be a steersman rather than an oarsman. How hard it is to continue pulling your oar to the beat of the drum when you know you are called to replace the person issuing the orders. How excruciating it can be when you are required to keep on happily serving a man who is driven by performance, workaholism, a slavery mindset when you know you are called to be royalty! Yet this is what God expected of David. He expected him to learn to go low before he would allow him to be lifted high.

In 1 Peter 2:5, we read these words: "Clothe yourselves, all of you, with humility towards one another." Learning to be humble doesn't disqualify us from promotion. It paces the way for it. Humility is the soil in which your heroism grows. Without first learning humility, you can never exercise authority. As Andrew Murray once put it:

"Men sometimes speak as if humility and meekness would rob

us of what is noble and bold and manlike. O, that all would believe that this is the nobility of the kingdom of heaven, that this is the royal spirit that the King of heaven displayed, that this is Godlike, to humble oneself, to become the servant of all!"

If you're in the second chair for a season, welcome to your destiny! Many, many men have this experience every day, serving bosses in the workplace. The Bible never told us to obey these employers and managers, these apostles and pastors, *provided they are emotionally healthy!* There's no condition added to protect you from serving under toxic people! Your task is not to heal your boss; it's to serve him! The leader is responsible for their soul care, not you. He is responsible for self-leadership, not you. In other words, it is his duty to learn to lead himself first, others second. This is not your mission!

We may sit at our desks, head in hands, wondering why we need to serve in a galley where the captain is a harsh taskmaster. We may be bewildered by the fact that we are called for a season to serve someone who is complex, controlling and compulsive. We may wonder why God doesn't simply come and remove him or release him! But this is not ours to worry about, work towards or waste time trying to manipulate. Our role is to respect the position that person occupies. As oarsmen, our role is to be humble and accountable.

As so often, the devotional writer Andrew Murray puts it very clearly: "Here is the path to the higher life: down, lower down! Just as water always seeks and fills the lowest place, so the moment God finds men abased and empty, His glory and power flow in to exalt and to bless."

I have interviewed hundreds of applicants over the years for various roles and positions within business, church and education. While skill and education are important, the greatest virtue I look for is a condition of the heart. You can train skill and educate the mind, but very rarely can you change the heart to become teachable, loyal and accountable.

Humility is an exceptional virtue. If courage is the *highest* virtue, humility is the *foundational* virtue. Without building a foundation of humility and accountability in your life, you'll never see the other virtues grow in your heart.

Know this. If you get in the galley and row, you will begin to cultivate the fruit of the Spirit that is humility and it will start the moment you put your hand to the oar. No one ever said or promised it was going to be easy.

My friends, it's time to get in the galley and row!

> **QUOTE**
>
> *You cannot be a leader and ask other people to follow you unless you know how to follow too.*
>
> Sam Rayburn

CHAPTER 3 | MEN UNDER AUTHORITY

QUESTIONS

1. Have you spent time serving someone else's vision?

2. What positive lessons have you learned while sitting in the second chair?

3. Have you learned to worship God in the wilderness?

4. Which of the nine fruits of the Spirit is God cultivating in your right now?

5. Are you a man under authority?

6. Have you ever had to serve an emotionally unhealthy leader or manager?

7. What life lessons have you learned during this season?

THE 7 VALUES OF THOSE WHO GET IN THE GALLEY AND ROW

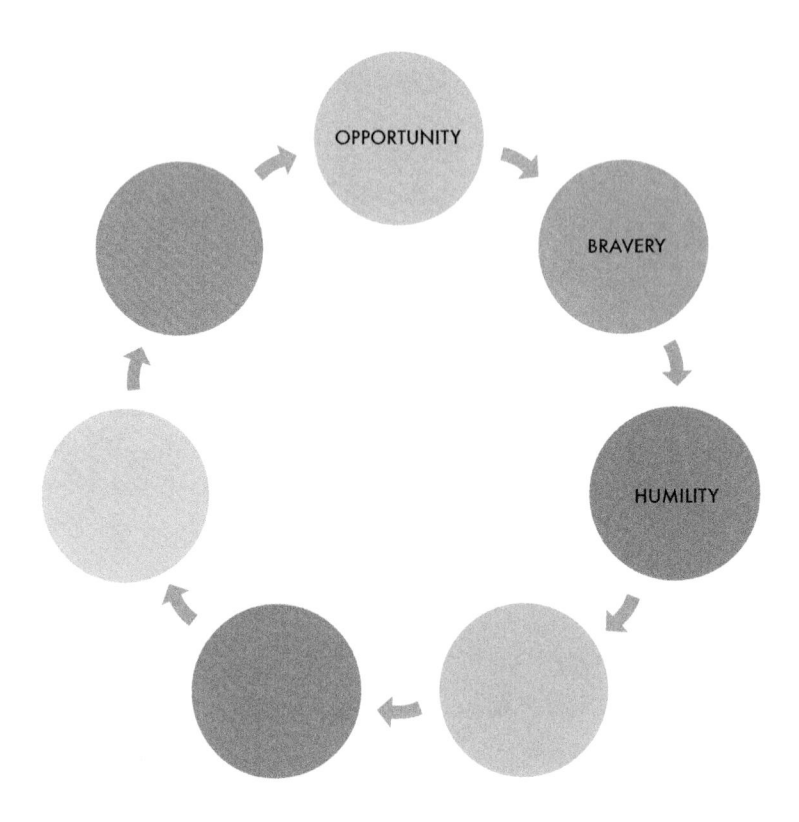

- OPPORTUNITY
- BRAVERY
- HUMILITY

---

[1] For the terminology of "yesterday's man" (Saul) and "today's man," see RT Kendall. https://www.premierchristianity.com/Past-Issues/2016/August-2016/How-not-to-become-yesterday-s-man-or-woman

CHAPTER 4

NO SLACKERS ALLOWED!

In Chapter 1, I told the story about how John Wesley went to the USA and was caught in a storm on board his ship. He thought he was going to die, and this brought him to the realisation that he didn't have any real assurance that he was going to heaven. Two years later, after a period of seeking God, the fire of the Holy Spirit filled his heart. His heart, he was to say, "was strangely warmed." Wesley, from this moment on, was a man in love with God.

Did this mean that he settled for a life of ease? The answer is an emphatic no! Both he and his brother Charles Wesley worked hard for the rest of their lives, serving the purpose of God in their generation. If it hadn't been for the tireless industry of these two men, and an eloquent preacher called George Whitefield, there would have been a guillotine in Hyde Park and people would have been singing the Marseillaise, not the National Anthem in Great Britain.

Let's take John Wesley's work output, first.

Did you know that he travelled 250,000 miles during his lifetime, mostly on horseback, so that he could preach the Gospel wherever he found an open door of opportunity? Have you ever ridden on a horse for a long time? It's uncomfortable! Those miles add up to about ten times around the globe, following the line of the equator! It is estimated that he preached 40,000 sermons during these journeys. That, I think you'll agree, is an example of commitment.

Then let's take Charles Wesley's output.

We've most of us sung some of his hymns. Let's just look at one of them. You'll have heard it even if you've not sung it.

And can it be that I should gain
An interest in the Savior's blood?
Died He for me, who caused His pain—
For me, who Him to death pursued?
Amazing love! How can it be,
That Thou, my God, shouldst die for me?

Refrain:

Amazing love! How can it be,
That Thou, my God, shouldst die for me?

'Tis myst'ry all: th' Immortal dies:
Who can explore His strange design?
In vain the firstborn seraph tries
To sound the depths of love divine.
'Tis mercy all! Let earth adore,
Let angel minds inquire no more.

He left His Father's throne above—
So free, so infinite His grace—
Emptied Himself of all but love,
And bled for Adam's helpless race:
'Tis mercy all, immense and free,
For, O my God, it found out me!

Long my imprisoned spirit lay,
Fast bound in sin and nature's night;
Thine eye diffused a quick'ning ray—
I woke, the dungeon flamed with light;
My chains fell off, my heart was free,
I rose, went forth, and followed Thee.

No condemnation now I dread;

CHAPTER 4 | NO SLACKERS ALLOWED!

Jesus, and all in Him, is mine;
Alive in Him, my living Head,
And clothed in righteousness divine,
Bold I approach th' eternal throne,
And claim the crown, through Christ my own.

Some say this is the greatest ever Christian hymn. Have you any idea how much hard work it takes to write something this profound, this beautiful, this all-encompassing? Maybe you think that it just fell from heaven into Charles Wesley's heart! But it didn't. Charles wrote it to celebrate his conversion in May 1738. It took him three days to complete it. Perspiration was needed as well as inspiration. And at the end of those three days, his brother John was saved too.

No one should underestimate the hard work involved, and this is just one hymn! Charles Wesley was very ill in the days before he began to compose it. On Pentecost Sunday 1738, he was convalescing in John Bray's home when he heard the man's sister say these words, "In the name of Jesus of Nazareth, arise, and believe, and thou shalt be healed of thy infirmities." Charles got out of bed and, reading the Psalms, was overwhelmed when he saw these words:

He hath put a new song in my mouth, even praise unto our God!

Psalm 40:3

This was not just Charles' moment of conversion and healing. It was also the wellspring for his hymn writing. In the next three days, he wrote two hymns, including *And Can it Be?*

In the half century that followed, he wrote another 8987, many of which are sung in churches today all over the world! He averaged ten lines of poetry a day for fifty years. In all, he composed ten times more than the next most prolific hymn writer of all time, Isaac Watts. He produced 56 volumes of hymns in 53 years! And these songs and hymns were things of unusual glory. A contemporary of his said this: "the song of the Methodists is the most beautiful I have ever heard." Another man described Charles as "the greatest hymn-writer of all ages."

Saved To Good Works

It's good to celebrate Charles Wesley because he's often been described as the "forgotten Wesley," being somewhat in his brother John's shadow. It's also good to celebrate him because he's an example of what happens to a man when he falls in love with Jesus. Far from becoming inactive and lazy, Charles worked harder than any composer in history to ensure that he wrote hymns that celebrated the wonders of Jesus Christ.

This is something immensely significant, especially in our generation where there is a mindset in the Church that tempts people into idleness. This mindset is based on the dangerous notion that all I need to do is say the sinner's prayer, be converted, and then go to heaven when I die.

This is the worst kind of deception!

There is nothing in the Bible to support this. Of course, we are never saved *by* our good works. But according to the Epistle of James in the New Testament, we are saved *to* good works. In other words, the man who has a *living* faith is the man who does everything within his power to bring heaven to those who are experiencing hell on earth.

The saved man seeks to communicate the good news about Jesus.

He seeks to feed the hungry and clothe the naked,

To see orphans set in families,

Widows defended and supported,

To fight injustice wherever it is found,

And to use his skills to change the world for the better.

He seeks to bring God's healing to the sick

And God's freedom to the oppressed.

He works hard to serve the Lord,

CHAPTER 4 | NO SLACKERS ALLOWED!

To fulfil God's purpose,

To use his gifts for God's glory

And to extend the kingdom of heaven on earth.

The truly saved man will therefore never sit back and claim that he needs to do nothing because he has his eternal life insurance sorted. No, just as a man in love will climb any mountain and cross any ocean for his beloved, so the Christian man cannot conceive of love being confined to words and not expressed in action. As James puts it,

Real religion, the kind that passes muster before God the Father, is this: Reach out to the homeless and loveless in their plight, and guard against corruption from the godless world.

James 1:27, (The Message).

You can no more show me your works apart from your faith than I can show you my faith apart from my works. Faith and works, works and faith, fit together hand in glove.

James 2:18, (The Message).

The very moment you separate body and spirit, you end up with a corpse. Separate faith and works and you get the same thing: a corpse.

James 2:26 (The Message)

Rowing is Hard Work!

Remember what the Apostle Paul said of David? "David served the purpose of God in his generation, then he fell asleep." David didn't say, "I believe in God, and that's enough for me to get to heaven when I die." He didn't say, "I've made a profession of faith, now I can sit back and enjoy the rest of my life." No, he believed in God, sure, but he also then proved that his was a *living* as opposed to a *dead* faith by working extremely hard for the rest of his days to do the things that God wanted him to do. Then he fell asleep, a beautiful euphemism for David's departure from this world in death.

The trouble with so many people today is that they think that they can rest and sleep after they've decided to believe in Jesus, rather than at the end of a purpose-driven and productive life of serving God. This is not a Biblical attitude, as we can see from David's life. David worked incredibly hard for God all his days. He didn't take the Western, consumerist view that believing in Jesus is all we need to do. His faith resulted in him writing psalms and ruling the nation of Israel – work that was necessary in his generation, work that only David was called to do and indeed capable of doing.

By now, I'm sure, you've got it! When Paul says that David served the purposes of God, he uses a naval metaphor. He says that David, believing that God had a purpose that was uniquely his to fulfil, seized the opportunity presented to himself, went down to the docks, volunteered to serve on board God's galley, climbed below decks, and started to row. And he went on rowing until the end of his life, whereupon he fell asleep. Well, you would wouldn't you? Rowing is hard work. Row for a couple of hours and you'll need a rest. Row for a lifetime and you'll need a long and refreshing sleep!

Let me introduce you to another James.

This time, not a New Testament letter writer, but an Olympic rower and British gold medallist.

His name is James Cracknell.

James said this in 2014: "When I first mentioned that I fancied having a go at rowing as a kid, no one bothered to tell me the suffering it would involve… I loved being on the water (once I'd mastered the art of not ending up *in* the water) and I found rowing gave me a feeling of freedom unlike anything I'd experienced before – but even that didn't match the sheer pleasure of winning, which I soon encountered in competitions. Rowing is an endurance sport and winning comes from hard training, so you have to go through a lot of physical pain and misery to pick up the medals. It's worth it, though."

We should take this seriously. If you've ever rowed as a sport,

CHAPTER 4 | NO SLACKERS ALLOWED!

you'll know that James is right. Rowing requires everything of us. It demands total physical fitness. It also demands 100% mental focus and concentration. Nothing comes easily to the rower. Success is the result of unparalleled passion and dedication. It does not come to the idle. It comes only to the industrious.

God Hates Laziness, Fact!

A good friend of mine, Mark Stibbe, was recently commissioned to write the devotional commentary on the Book of Proverbs for the Passion Translation of the Bible. As he went through the entire book, in this dynamic new version, he saw for the first time how angry our Heavenly Father gets when people are lazy. He pointed out that there are as many verses condemning the sluggard as there are the adulterer in Proverbs.

We all know that God hates adultery. That's clear from the Book of Proverbs too. Listen to this: "Don't be so stupid as to think you can get away with your adultery. It will destroy your life, and you'll pay the price for the rest of your days" (Proverbs 6:32). Those are harsh words and a grave warning for all of us! We'll have cause to come back to them when we look later at the story of David and Bathsheba.

But did you know that God gets as mad about laziness as he does about adultery in Proverbs? In the old versions of the Bible, this person is known as the Sluggard. In the Passion Translation, he's known as the Slacker. God hates slackers. He roundly condemns idleness.

You want some proof?

Here's Proverbs 10:4. "Slackers will know what it means to be poor, while the hard worker becomes wealthy." Nothing could be clearer than this! You want to enjoy prosperity? Then work hard! Nothing comes to the lazy. There is no reward for the idle.

Here's Proverbs 12:11, "Work hard at your job and you'll have what you need. Following a get-rich-quick scheme is nothing but a fantasy." In other words, don't gamble, a growing national problem in the UK. Don't do the lottery. Far too many people are trying to get rich quick by doing as little work as possible.

Here's Proverbs 13:4: "The slacker wants it all and ends up with nothing,

but the hard worker ends up with all that he longed for." How true this is to life! Time and again you see the hard worker meeting their basic needs. Not just their needs, but the needs of their family too.

Being lazy is a sign that you're behaving like an orphan, operating with a spirit of entitlement, expecting everything for nothing. Being a hard worker is a sign that you're behaving like a son, doing everything you can to put food on the table for your family. As it says in Proverbs 10:5, "What a waste when an incompetent son sleeps through his day of opportunity!" Sleeping is what you do *after* you've served God's purpose for your generation.

If you're lazy, you'll sleep while the opportunity of a lifetime is upon you, missing your moment because of laziness.

If you're awake and hardworking, you'll seize the day.

Remember what Proverbs teaches: the orphan is a man of idleness.

The son is a man of industry.

The son is a rower on the galley of the Lord.

The Singing King

Charles Wesley wasn't the only one who wrote great songs. King David did too. Right from the earliest days, David found himself singing to God while he looked after his father's sheep on the hills. When he became King of Israel, he didn't stop singing. Far from

CHAPTER 4 | NO SLACKERS ALLOWED!

it. He composed many of the Psalms while he was busy governing a nation through times of great change. This is because for King David, expressing his adoration was the most important priority in his life. Before David was a leader of people, he was a lover of God. Before he was a warrior, he was a worshipper. Nothing was more important.

We all know Psalm 23; it begins with the beautiful image of God as a shepherd, protecting and caring for us, his sheep – an image that was inspired by David's youth, when he was a shepherd too:

The LORD is my shepherd, I lack nothing.
He makes me lie down in green pastures,
he leads me beside quiet waters,
he refreshes my soul.

The Psalm ends with a lyrical expression of hope – the hope that one day David will find himself in the Father's house in heaven, spending eternity in the presence of the Shepherd King:

Surely your goodness and love will follow me
all the days of my life,
and I will dwell in the house of the LORD
forever.

Do you know what it takes to write poetry of this calibre? Do you have any idea how many hours of dedicated skill are needed to produce a song of this memorable and lasting quality? Yes, David had the anointing of the Holy Spirit and relied on that for his inspiration. But the Holy Spirit requires our human collaboration. We are not just keyboards on which he types. We are people whose skills he uses, whose experiences he enlists.

This means work! It means spending hours and hours, days and days, honing your craft and refining what you create. Yes, God's power was at work in David's life. But David's craft was important too. This craft was not the product of idleness but industry. It flowed out of a lifetime of writing and composing, all to the glory of God.

Out of this hard work, the Book of Psalms emerged, a stunning collection of songs, the majority of which are attributed to David. These cover the whole of our spiritual lives – the past, the present and the future. They deal with the entire gamut of our emotional life with God – our sighs, our sobs and our songs. They also celebrate the qualities of God in a comprehensive and heartfelt way: his eternity, faithfulness, goodness, glory, omnipresence, omniscience, omnipotence, mercy, majesty, holiness, justice, care, uniqueness and love, to name just a few of his divine attributes. No wonder the key word in the Psalms is "praise", used 211 times. Praise was as important as breathing to David.

All this was part of David's rowing! Below decks in God's galley, David composed and sang songs – songs that were not just to be sung by him but by everyone who signs up to serve God's purpose in their generation. As we pull on the oars with our hands, we let the songs pour from our hearts. We sing together. We sing in harmonies. We sing to the beat of God's drum, allowing God to set the rhythm and the tempo.

Imagine a world without Psalm 23! In just about every funeral you will go to, you will either hear these words read out loud, or you will sing them. What would have happened if David had said, on the day the Holy spirit wanted to anoint him with creativity, "I can't be bothered"? What if David had chosen idleness instead of industry?

Without Psalm 23, and the Psalms of David generally, we would have been denied one of the richest treasures in the Bible – a treasury of praise that inspires our own worship of God. As C.S. Lewis once wrote, "The most valuable thing the Psalms do for me is to express the same delight in God which made David dance." As Charles Spurgeon testified: "The delightful study of the Psalms has yielded me boundless profit and ever-growing pleasure."

Thank God for David's industry

CHAPTER 4 | NO SLACKERS ALLOWED!

No Shoddy Workmanship Here!

Another poet provides a warning for us as I draw this chapter to a close, Samuel Taylor Coleridge, who wrote most of his works in the years just after Charles Wesley died. If Charles Wesley was the man of industry, Coleridge was in many ways a man of idleness. Although his output is still significant, some of his life was lived in a dejected, inactive and often drug-addicted state. Consequently, many of the things he started, he failed to finish.

The finest 20th century commentaries on the books of the Bible were written by William Barclay and he wrote about Coleridge's lack of industry in his interpretation of Matthew chapter 7. His words are a stark warning to all of us not to become sluggards or slackers.

"Coleridge," Barclay reflected, "is the supreme tragedy of indiscipline. Never did so great a mind produce so little. He left Cambridge University to join the army; he left the army because, in spite of all his erudition, he could not rub down a horse; he returned to Oxford and left without a degree. He began a paper called *The Watchman* which lived for ten numbers and then died. It has been said of him: 'He lost himself in visions of work to be done, that always remained to be done. Coleridge had every poetic gift but one--the gift of sustained and concentrated effort.' In his head and in his mind he had all kinds of books, as he said, himself, 'completed save for transcription.' "I am on the eve," he says, "of sending to the press two octave volumes." But the books were never composed outside Coleridge's mind, because. he would not face the discipline of sitting down to write them out. No one ever reached any eminence, and no one having reached it ever maintained it, without discipline."

Benjamin Franklin, another fine writer, once said this, "energy and persistence conquer all things." I believe this to be profoundly true. No one ever succeeded as an oarsman in the Roman navy without effort, and no galley in the Roman navy ever conquered their enemies without a crew committed to energy and persistence. As Admiral McRaven (former Navy Seal) once observed, "If you want to change the world, start off by making your bed!"

Whatever we do, we need to do whole-heartedly, working as hard as we can. As the Apostle Paul wrote in Colossians 3:23-25,

Servants, do what you're told by your earthly masters. And don't just do the minimum that will get you by. Do your best. Work from the heart for your real Master, for God, confident that you'll get paid in full when you come into your inheritance. Keep in mind always that the ultimate Master you're serving is Christ. The sullen servant who does shoddy work will be held responsible. Being a follower of Jesus doesn't cover up bad work.

Soli Deo Gloria

That said, I don't want to end on a negative note. Let me conclude by talking about another composer whose industry was immense and whose output was extraordinary. I'm talking about Johan Sebastian Bach, who composed his music in the same century that Charles Wesley wrote his hymns.

Surprisingly little is known about Bach's life, but we do know that he was a Christian. The evidence for this is his three-volume study Bible which is covered extensively by his personal notes. All three volumes are inscribed "J.S. Bach. 1733." Experts have confirmed that it is in his handwriting.

This study Bible not only contained the text of the Holy Scriptures, it also included a commentary by a man greatly influenced by the sermons of Martin Luther. We can infer from this that Bach loved Martin Luther's theology, and that he, like Luther, he had been saved by believing in Jesus.

Bach believed that he was called to preach the Good News about Jesus *through* music. Indeed, he believed that the more perfectly his devotional music was realised, the more listeners would encounter

CHAPTER 4 | NO SLACKERS ALLOWED!

Jesus through his compositions. As a result, to many, he is known as "the Fifth Evangelist."

Bach worked tirelessly to produce magnificent masterpieces like his sublime choral work *St Matthew's Passion*, and he did so because, as he wrote next to 2 Chronicles 5:13 in his Bible, "At a reverent performance of music, God is always at hand with his gracious presence."

In all this, Bach worked hard, showing unrelenting dedication. In his formative years, aged 20, he once walked 280 miles to Northern Germany to hear a concert, so determined was he to hear the organ music of a celebrated composer. In all, he wrote over 1000 compositions.

Sometimes, Bach used his craft to compose frivolous pieces. One noteworthy example is the song he wrote about coffee, a drink which he loved. It goes like this:

> Ah! How sweet coffee tastes
> More delicious than a thousand kisses
> Milder than muscatel wine.
> Coffee, I have to have coffee,
> And, if someone wants to pamper me,
> Ah, then bring me coffee as a gift!

Many of us, I suspect, can relate to the sentiments of that song!

That said, Bach is best known for the extraordinary choral works he wrote in praise of the death of Christ – *The Passion of St John* and *The Passion of St Matthew*. These works show his utter dedication to Christ and his faith in the finished work of the Cross. And here's the thing. All this was the product of industry or hard work. And all this was all done for the glory of God.

What's the evidence for this?

At the top of many of his original musical scores, you can find the following in his handwriting. I.N.J. This is an abbreviation of the Latin phrase, *in nominee Jesus*, "in the name of Jesus."

At the bottom of these original scores (sheets of music) you can find Bach writing the following, S.D.G. This is an abbreviation of the Latin phrase, *Soli Deo Gloria*, "to the glory of God alone."

Bach said, "The main purpose of my music is to glorify God. Some people do this with music that is simple. I haven't chosen to use a simple style, but my music comes from my heart as a humble offering to God. This honours God no matter what musical style I use."

Perhaps you can see now why Bach prayed a beautiful and humble prayer every time he started to compose a piece of music (often church music). "Jesus, help me show your glory through the music I write. May it bring you joy even as it brings joy to your people."

Whatever we do, when we volunteer to serve God's purpose in our generation, we sign up for industry and hard work, but we do it all as unto the Lord, in the Lord's name, and to the Lord's glory alone.

That is the true spirit of the Christian under-rower!

Soli Deo Gloria!

To the Glory of God Alone!

My friends, it's time to get in the galley and row!

> **QUOTE**
> *Big tasks usually go to the men who prove their ability to outgrow small ones.*
>
> **Theodore Roosevelt**

CHAPTER 4 | NO SLACKERS ALLOWED!

QUESTIONS

1. Is your faith in Christ expressed through working hard for him?

2. Are you like an Olympic Rower, giving 100% to the cause?

3. Have you ever seen laziness as a sin?

4. Are you living a life of industry or indolence?

5. Are there any areas of your life right now where you could be accused of being a "slacker"?

6. Are you, like Bach, studying the Scriptures deeply and daily?

7. In what ways is the hard work you're doing bringing glory to God?

THE 7 VALUES OF THOSE WHO GET IN THE GALLEY AND ROW

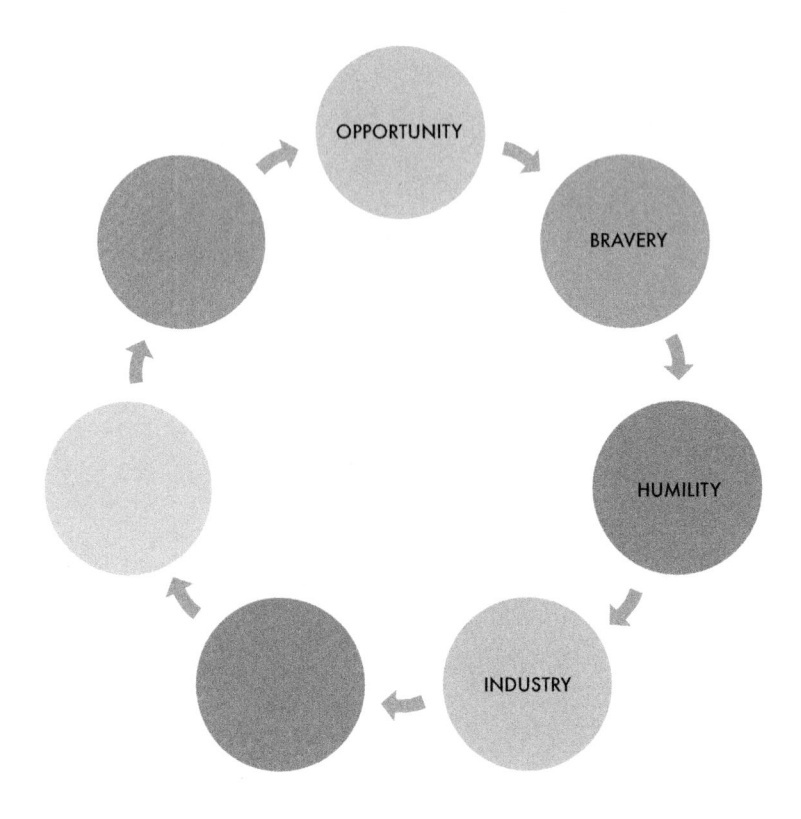

- OPPORTUNITY
- BRAVERY
- HUMILITY
- INDUSTRY

CHAPTER 5

ROWING IN UNISON

One of the greatest Christian men in history is someone whose name many of you reading this may never heard. I'm talking about Jeremiah Lanphier, the man who was responsible for lighting the fire that started the greatest revival New York City has ever witnessed and one of the greatest moves of God in history - the Great Prayer Awakening in 1857-8 in the USA.

It all started when Jeremiah – who incidentally was a businessman not a clergyman - became deeply distressed by the decline in the Christian faith in the city and in the nation. Americans had become disillusioned with Christianity after a man had prophesied that Jesus would return in 1844. When the date passed without note, many of the population of the country – at that time numbering 30 million – fell away from the faith, drifting into spiritual apathy. Seeing this run its course for over a decade, Jeremiah felt prompted to call fellow businessmen in New York to prayer. Put in the language of this book, he decided to seize the opportunity of a lifetime in the lifetime of that opportunity (chapter 1). He decided to be courageous and to do something about the state of spiritual lethargy that had infected the city (chapter 2). He humbled himself by choosing to call people to express their utter dependence on God (chapter 3). And he worked tirelessly and faithfully to see his vision become a reality (chapter 4). Opportunity led to bravery. Bravery led to humility. Humility led to industry.

Jeremiah's publicised his first prayer meeting for Wednesday lunchtime September 23rd 1857 in the Dutch Reformed Church on Fulton Street in New York. Jeremiah was thinking outside the box here. He wasn't calling for a Sunday morning meeting for regular church members, led by a minister. He was calling for a midweek, Wednesday lunchtime meeting for working men, and one led by laymen not clergymen. As Jeremiah put it: "This meeting is intended to give merchants, mechanics, clerks, strangers, and businessmen generally an opportunity to stop and call upon God amid the perplexities incident to their respective avocations. It will continue for one hour; but it is also designed for those who may find it inconvenient to remain more than five or ten minutes, as well as for those who can spare the whole hour."

Straightaway, we can see perhaps why such a meeting appealed to men. It was during the working day, in their lunchbreak. It was not a lengthy evening meeting with long prayers and excessive emotions. It was a calm, accessible meeting in which you could opt in for six or sixty minutes, depending on your commitments in the workplace.

So then, what happened?

When Jeremiah began at noon September 23rd, no one showed up.

Five minutes went by and still no one.

Ten, fifteen, twenty, twenty-five minutes.

No one came.

At half past the hour, the first man arrived. By the end of the meeting, there were six of them all, all from different denominations, all praying together for a revival of true Christianity in the city and the nation.

The following Wednesday, September 30th, there were forty.

Within six months, there were ten thousand praying all over the city. Within two years, there were one million new converts and one million recommitments to a living Christian faith. In fact, there were some towns in the USA where you couldn't find a single non-Christian and the ice on the Mohawk River had to be broken with axes, so great was the cry for baptisms. Most powerful of all, ships coming into harbour at New York City where so impacted by the holy presence of God that entire crews were falling on their faces, repenting of sin, putting their trust in Jesus, and finding themselves born again. The Layman's Prayer revival, as it is sometimes called, swept through the city and the country, and from the USA to Great Britain, Scandinavia and even as far as India.

All because one man decided to get in the galley and row.

They Prayed with One Heart

When we look to find the key to this remarkable move of God, it's not long before we find it. It was **unity**. The six men who gathered in that very first meeting belonged to different denominations. They put aside all differences and prayed with one accord for people to come to Christ. This trans-denominational unity continued throughout the following two years as prayer meetings spread like wildfire throughout the country. The former divisions no longer mattered. Engaged as they were in one common vision, old dividing walls came crashing down and new bridges were built.

So then, what was this common vision? Outside the prayer meetings, there was a poster that exhorted visitors to avoid all controversial topics in their prayers. The focus was on praying for the salvation of family members, friends, neighbours and work colleagues. Nothing else was allowed. Everyone had to stay on topic. People who wanted to pray about other matters were politely told not to pray in the meetings for those concerns and to take them elsewhere, to more appropriate gatherings. Everyone was told to row in the same direction. Everyone was urged to hold fast to the heavenly vision and to stay on course.

This brought remarkable results.

One man, far from God, wandered into one of the meetings. As people were praying for one man's soul, he realised that they were praying for him. His mother, as it turned out, had written his name on a note and handed it in at the meeting. The men got praying for him, little realising that he was somehow, miraculously, in the same room. Not surprisingly, it wasn't long before he gave his life to Christ.

All this is reminiscent of the prayer meetings in the Book of Acts where we often read that the people participating would intercede "with one accord." The word translated "one accord" is *homothumadon* in Greek. It comes from *homo* meaning 'the same' and *thumos* meaning 'glow', 'ardour', 'passion'. What characterised the prayer meetings of the first Christians was their unity. They were all singing from the same hymn sheet.

No wonder the fire of God's presence fell upon them!

No wonder people felt the manifest and white-hot presence of God!

No wonder sinners and seekers found their way to Christ!

We see the same thing in Jeremiah Lanphier's day.

People got united in praying and the glory of the Lord appeared inside and outside the churches – even at sea!

Some of the reports from the time are simply stunning. This is from March 1858: "The large cities and towns from Maine to California are sharing in this great and glorious work. There is hardly a village or town to be found where 'a special divine power' does not appear displayed."

One man attended a meeting of 4000 men in Jayne's Hall in Philadelphia. He wrote, "I have never, I think, been present at a more stirring and edifying prayer meeting, the room quite full, and a divine influence seemed manifest. Many hearts melted. Many souls devoutly engaged."

CHAPTER 5 | ROWING IN UNISON

All this flowed from the complete unity of those praying. Unity, in fact, was the watchword in this tremendous revival. Samuel Prime, who witnessed this move of God in 1857-8, and who wrote an inspiring book-length account of it, said this of the meetings:

"Christians of both sexes, of all ages, of different denominations, without the slightest regard to denominational distinctions, came together, on one common platform of brotherhood in Christ, and in the bonds of Christian union sent up their united petitions to the throne of the heavenly giver.

The question was never asked, 'To what church does he belong?' But the question was, 'Does he belong to Christ?'

This union of Christians in prayer struck the unbelieving world with amazement. It was felt that this was prayer. This love of Christians for one another, and this love of Christ, this love of prayer and love of souls, this union of all in prayer, whose names were lost sight of, disarmed all opposition, so that not a man opened his mouth in opposition."

What a testimony!

And what unity!

There really is no limit to what God can do in a town, city or nation when men get rowing together with one heart and one voice, pulling on their oars at the same time, following together the beat of the same drum.

A Commanded Blessing

The life of King David is another great example of this beautiful value of unity. As we've seen, when Paul said that David served God's purpose, he used a nautical metaphor, indicating that David became an under-rower in God's galley. If there's one thing you know about these ships it's this: they were made up of many rowers, not just one. Some had only one deck of rowers and were called *monoremes*. Others two decks and were termed *biremes*. A few had three decks and were known as *triremes*. You get the picture? Men rowed together, not alone.

David understood that no man will ever succeed in serving God's purpose if he goes it alone. Consequently, he had a passion for unity. Strategically, we can see this in the way he sought to unify his nation – a plan that we'll look at in more detail later. David knew that the strength of his people lay in their integration not their fragmentation. As I've written in another book, "the devil isolates, but Jesus integrates." Jesus prayed for our complete unity in John 17. When we are truly one, the world is astounded, the devil is confounded.

But David's passion for unity was not just his politics, it was his prayer. In the last chapter, we celebrated his industry, his extraordinary commitment to finding the time and the space in an already busy life to compose what we call the Psalms. Many of these are the result of David's personal creativity. They are poetic expressions of his very real and sometimes raw relationship with his Heavenly Father. In one of these Psalms, he gives voice to the passion for unity that burned like an unstoppable wildfire within his soul.

> *How truly wonderful and delightful*
> *to see brothers and sisters living together in sweet unity!*
> *It's as precious as the sacred scented oil*
> *flowing from the head of the high priest Aaron,*
> *dripping down upon his beard and running all the way down*
> *to the hem of his priestly robes.*
> *This heavenly harmony can be compared to the dew*
> *dripping down from the skies upon Mount Hermon,*
> *refreshing the mountain slopes of Israel.*
> *For from this realm of sweet harmony*
> *God will release his eternal blessing, the promise of life forever!*

(Psalm 133, The Passion Translation)

What a tremendous celebration of the value of unity. In *The*

Passion Translation, this psalm is introduced as "a song to bring you higher." Do you feel like you've been taken higher reading that? I do!

Why does David believe so ardently in the value of unity? An older translation gives the answer in these words: "For there the Lord has *commanded* the blessing" (RSV, Psalm 133:3). When we dwell in complete unity together as brothers, there the Lord promises us that he will authorise his blessing, which is the promise of *life*.

Do you want to see revival – new life in the Holy Spirit?

Then set your heart on the Davidic value of unity.

Set your heart on rowing together, not rowing alone.

The Mystery of Synergy

As soon as a man signed up to be an under-rower in the Roman navy, he committed himself to serving in a community. In that onboard group, unity was essential. Everyone needed to know their place and their role on the galley, and everyone needed to work together in unison.

The man in charge of the direction of the ship was **the steersman** and he listened carefully to **the lookout**. Then there was **the chief oarsman**, and he set the pace using **the drummer** and **a flute player**. In addition, there was **a doctor**, a team of **master carpenters**, a **quarter master** and a troop of **archers**.

Most important of all, there were **the oarsmen**, the *remiges* as they were called in Latin. When these rowers were rowing in time, pulling together in an unspoiled unity, the distances covered and the speeds attained were quite breath-taking, even by modern standards.

A recent study has revealed that these oarsmen were capable of feats of strength that no modern athlete can match. One trireme (with three banks of 170 oarsmen) rowed non-stop for 24 hours at a speed of seven knots, preventing a massacre on the island of Lesbos. When a team of modern oarsmen tried to repeat this performance in a reconstructed trireme, they got nowhere near these levels. This experiment took place before the 2004 Olympics and the rowers in question were some of the fittest athletes in the world. An expert physiologist, Dr Rossiter, told New Scientist magazine: "It was clear that a sustained seven knots was outside the aerobic capacity of the modern oarsmen."

What we're talking about here is not just the far greater athletic prowess of ancient oarsmen, but also the mystery of *synergy*. In rowing, synergy is defined as follows: the sum of the total crew of oarsmen is greater than the total sum of each individual rower. Rowing synergy is measured by a crew's ability to outperform even its best individual rower. Winning crews are those whose high performances are the result of synergy, of working together at such a level of unity that they even beat crews where the individual rowers are better on paper.

When high-performing rowers work as individuals, then the equation looks something like this (when the crew is a compliment of four):

1 + 1 + 1 + 1 = less than 4

When the same crew works together rather than as individuals, then the equation looks very different:

1 + 1 + 1 + 1 = more than 4.

That's synergy!

What King David knew was this: when brothers live and work together in complete unity, there the Lord commands his blessing of life. What does that mean? It means that in addition to the *natural* synergy created by working as a team rather than as individuals, there is a *supernatural* synergy too. In other words, not only is the human energy astounding, but the divine energy – what we might the call the revival power of God – is truly awe-inspiring too. The anointing, as David says in Psalm 133, is experienced when we are one.

When we get in the galley and row, we row together!

When that happens, God adds his oil to our toil.

The Devil Divides

Perhaps you can see now why the devil's favourite tactic is "divide and rule." This strategy derives from the Latin phrase *divide et impera* and was a common practice in Roman times. The Romans knew all too well that the best way to reduce the power of an opposing army was to turn a large body of soldiers into much smaller units. When opponents are collectively united, they are far more powerful. When they are fragmented, and even at odds with each other, then victory is almost guaranteed in the ensuing fight.

This is true for naval battles too, as the following two stories attest. One night, two battleships spotted each other in the darkness. They fired a salvo at each other and, in the raging conflict that followed, many men were wounded and both vessels were severely damaged. When daylight broke the next dawn, both captains discovered to their horror that they were both flying the same English flag. They were on the same side!

This is what can happen in the darkness. Friends who would normally be allies can turn on each other.

Many years earlier, just before the battle of Trafalgar in 1805, the British naval hero Lord Nelson learned that an admiral and a captain in his fleet were not on good terms. Sending for the two men, he placed the hands of the admiral and the captain together. Then, looking them both in the face, he pointed to the French fleet and said, "Look! Yonder is the enemy!"

Nelson knew all too well that when people who are supposed to be fighting with each other start fighting against each other, the safety and the prosperity of the entire fleet can be compromised and even lost.

What a lesson! Sometimes, the devil infiltrates a church community and starts tempting people to fall out with each other. His tactics are usually vile and insidious whenever he does this.

When we give into the temptation to fall into gossip or even factions, the enemy has already won half the battle for control over the destiny of our church. Where there is unity, the Lord commands his blessing, even life for evermore. Where there is disunity, the devil has a field day. He causes us to miss out on serving God's purpose in our generation and in missing out on that we deny the lost an encounter with Jesus that is a matter of life and death.

That is truly tragic.

Eternal Destinies are at Stake

When we look again at Jeremiah Lanphier, we see a man who was prepared to get in the galley and row, and if we remind ourselves of the five values we've celebrated in this book so far, we can witness them all in his life.

Firstly, we see **opportunity**. Lanphier felt an urgency. He didn't know why. He just knew that something was troubling his spirit in the summer of 1857. He sensed that God was about to move. It was time to act.

Secondly, we see **bravery**. It would have been all too easy for him to say, "I'm not an ordained minister. Who am I?" But he didn't. He showed courage. He responded bravely to a dark and desperate situation.

Thirdly, we see **humility**. Jeremiah knew the difference between pride and humility. Pride is manifested in man's independence from God. Humility is expressed in man's utter dependence on God. The no 1 sign that men are starting to embrace true humility is that they get on their knees to pray, for what could be more indicative of the authentically humble heart than the yearning to engage in prevailing and travailing prayer. Men need to go low to ascend to such heights. That's humility, without doubt.

Fourthly, we see **industry**. No one can deny that Jeremiah worked hard in establishing and then sustaining these fervent prayer meetings that began in Fulton Street, New York. As they began to spread all over the country, and as the power of the Holy Spirit began to move for the salvation of many thousands of souls, the prayer meetings grew larger and more frequent. That meant work, but Jeremiah was not a man of idleness; he was a man of industry.

Finally, we see **unity**. The hallmark of the first prayer meeting, and every other meeting afterwards, was an extraordinary unity of people and purpose. This closing of ranks meant that opposition to the move of God all but disappeared. Even the press was supportive.

In summary: *Jeremiah Lanphier bravely volunteered to serve in the galley, humbly serving below decks, working hard and insisting on rowing in unison.*

He couldn't have known what would happen next.

Just days after the first prayer meeting, the stock exchange unexpectedly and suddenly crashed in New York city and many men went to bed financially secure only to awake the next day out of work and desperate. The prayer meetings that exploded across the country turned out to be their only hope in distressing times. For many, it was a matter of life and death. Remembering what really matters, they chose life. Eternal life.

And after the revival, the next great event in US history, following on immediately from this mighty move of God, was the American Civil war. It has been estimated by historians that hundreds of thousands of men who were swept into the kingdom in 1857-8 were then carried to heaven in the years that followed on the battlefields of America. Had it not been for these united prayer meetings, they would have died out of relationship with Christ.

That would have been the worst of tragedies.

So, remember what David said in Psalm 133. When there is true and heartfelt unity, God commands the blessing of life for ever with him, starting now but extending into eternity. If there had not been this remarkable depth of unity in 1857-8, men would have missed out on their eternal destinies.

Do you now see how precious unity is?

My friends, it's time to get in the galley and row!

And let's row together, because it's hard to rock the boat when you're too busy rowing it!

> **QUOTE**
>
> *Synergy is better than my way or your way. It's our way.*
>
> Stephen Covey

CHAPTER 5 | ROWING IN UNISON

QUESTIONS

1. Are you a man who serves Christ alone, or who serves Christ with other men?

2. Do you have a group of men with whom you pray regularly?

3. Do you have male friends with whom you can share your whole heart?

4. Are you praying with other men for revival?

5. Are you protecting the unity of all your relationships, including at home?

6. Do you know what it is to experience God's supernatural synergy?

7. Do you know what it is to live in God's "commanded blessing"?

THE 7 VALUES OF THOSE WHO GET IN THE GALLEY AND ROW

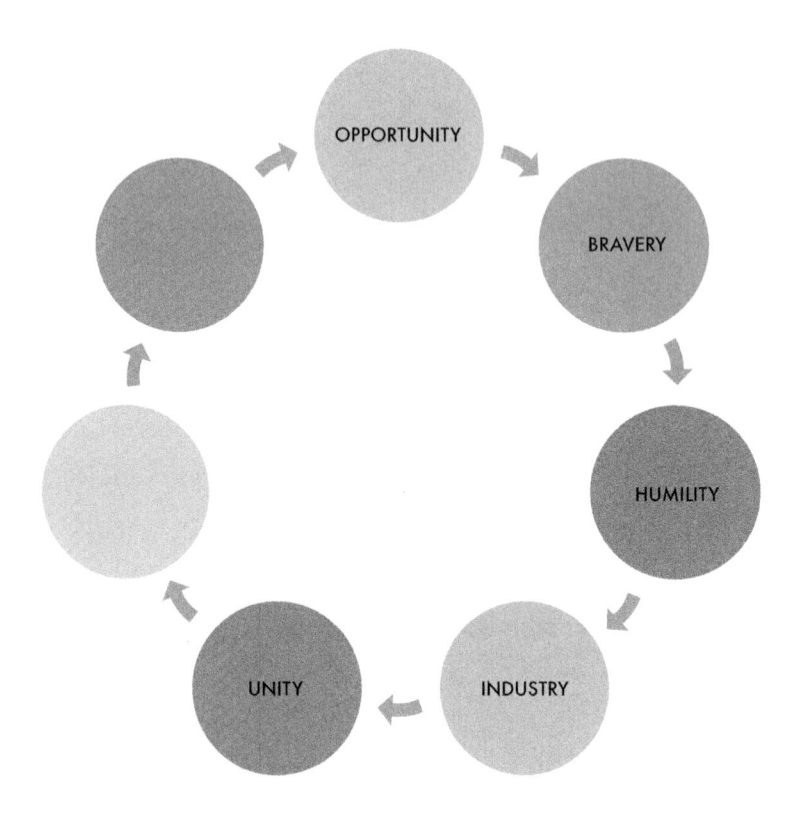

- OPPORTUNITY
- BRAVERY
- HUMILITY
- INDUSTRY
- UNITY

CHAPTER 6

MINDING THE GAP

Few people would argue with the claim that the greatest evangelist of the twentieth century was Billy Graham. He gave his life to Jesus at an early age and then dedicated the rest of his life to his Lord. He believed with all his heart that God could use anyone, even him. When he was relatively young, he said "When God gets ready to shake America, he may not take the Ph.D. and the D.D. God may choose a country boy … and I pray that he would!"

Well, he did! God used a country boy to preach live to over 80 million people. Add to this all the many more millions who heard him on the radio and through his TV and film ministry and the number becomes unquantifiable. At his crusades, it is estimated that he led over 3 million sinners to Christ. No wonder his public influence became so great. He became the spiritual advisor to every President who exercised authority during his life as an evangelist, whatever their religious persuasions or political beliefs. Almost every year since the 1950s until his recent death, Billy was voted among the top ten of America's most admired and respected men. When he died, America mourned.

There will never be another Billy Graham.

He stepped into the galley and rowed.

He served God's purpose in his generation.

Chief among the reasons for Billy's unparalleled success and untarnished reputation was his integrity. What is integrity? It is being the same person in public as you are in private. It is having the same level of moral authenticity on the podium as you have in the bedroom. As a Christian, Billy believed there should be no integrity gap. As Billy was fond of saying, "the true Christian is the man who can lend his pet parrot to the town gossip."

In 1948, Billy and his team were conducting a series of meetings in Modesto, Mexico, when he sat down with them to talk about integrity. They spent 24 hours discussing how they could maintain the highest possible integrity. Concerned that he should not be trapped into a moral fall, Billy established what are known as the four rules of his ministry. These four rules were intended to establish and sustain commitment and purity in all of them.

Rule 1: **Money**

The team agreed that they would not wring as much money as they could out of their audiences and that they would always be transparent and accountable when it came to money and accounts.

Rule 2: **Sex**

They all knew of evangelists who, separated from their families by travel, had fallen into sexual sin. Billy decided for the rest of his life he would never travel alone, or meet alone, with a woman not his wife.

Rule 3: **Independence**

Billy and his team all knew of evangelists who conducted their ministries without reference to local churches, often openly criticising local pastors. Billy resolved to work with local churches and their leaders in every city where he preached.

Rule 4: **Publicity**

Billy and his team resolved not to do what other evangelists do and exaggerate their successes or lie about attendance numbers and the number of conversions. They dedicated themselves to truth-telling in reporting.

CHAPTER 6 | MINDING THE GAP

These four rules became known as "The Modesto Manifesto" and Billy kept them until they end of his life. On no occasion was he found wanting in any of these four areas. He was not manipulative or dishonest with money. He did not compromise at any point in the area of sexual purity. He always ran crusades with the full support of local churches in the area. And he never lied or exaggerated about what he had seen and done.

That's integrity.

The Billy Graham Rule

In his magnificent autobiography *Just as I Am*, Billy talks about the second rule, the covenant to be sexually pure. Reflecting afterwards about the meeting in Modesto, and specifically the second rule, Billy said the following: "We all knew of evangelists who had fallen into immorality while separated from their families by travel. We pledged among ourselves to avoid any situation that would have even the appearance of compromise or suspicion. From that day on, I did not travel, meet or eat alone with a woman other than my wife. We determined that the Apostle Paul's mandate to the young pastor Timothy would be ours as well: 'Flee ... youthful lusts' (2 Timothy 1:22, KJV)."

This second rule, specifically the resolution never to travel alone with a woman not his wife, became famously known as "The Billy Graham Rule" because no one had made such a practical and radical step before in the area of sexual holiness. The reason why Billy was so intentional about this area was because he wanted to maintain the highest levels of *integrity*. As he said of the process and rationale of the Modesto Manifesto: "We made a series of resolutions or commitment among ourselves that would guide us in our future evangelistic work. In reality, it was more of an informal understanding among ourselves - a shared commitment to do all we could do to uphold *the Bible's standard of absolute integrity and purity* for evangelists" (Italics mine).

All this leads us back to the story of King David. Throughout this book we've been studying Paul's magnificent epitaph of David in Acts 13:38: "David served God's purpose in his generation and then he fell asleep." We've pointed out the beautiful naval metaphor behind the word "served," showing how David volunteered to serve below decks, seizing the **opportunity** of his lifetime, exhibiting great **bravery** right from the start, exercising **humility** in his apprenticeship in the service of King Saul, choosing **industry** rather than indolence, prioritizing **unity** rather than isolationism.

Looking at this list of qualities, it would be all too easy to idealise David. But the Bible won't let us do that. When you look at David's life, he did make mistakes, none more destructive than his affair with Bathsheba, in which he not only committed adultery, but also murder, breaking two of God's Ten Commandments in the process. For a time, David tried to cover up his sin, presenting himself as one thing in public, while living quite another reality in private. That's the integrity gap right there. But his sins eventually found him out. David was brought to his knees in the most heartfelt repentance.

But how did this destruction begin?

The opening verses of 2 Samuel 11 tell us.

In the spring, at the time when kings go off to war, David sent Joab out with the king's men and the whole Israelite army. They destroyed the Ammonites and besieged Rabbah. But David remained in Jerusalem.

Here lies one of the keys to David's loss of integrity. David was a warrior king. He was supposed to be out winning battles for God. It was the season for conquering enemies and taking ground. But instead, David stayed behind, letting others do the work. He chose indolence over industry. And it was this indolence, this refusal to work, this abstaining from war, that led to his downfall.

If there is a first lesson about integrity in this story, it's this: *when we become idle and bored, we set ourselves up as presentable targets for the enemy, especially in the area of sexual temptation.*

CHAPTER 6 | MINDING THE GAP

David's problem, then, was that he stopped working.

He had volunteered to serve in God's galley.

But he chose resting when he should have been rowing.

And in that moment, he gave the devil an opportunity.

When Good Men Fall

The context for David's sin is extremely important. It is a constant warning to men not to grow lazy and bored, because it in these moments that we are at our most vulnerable to temptation. Spending too much time in bed, either sleeping or awake, is – as the Book of Proverbs constantly admonishes us – a very dangerous thing. Not only does it cause us to miss out on the harvest. It also sets us up for temptation and sin.

See how it all proceeds with David:

One evening David got up from his bed and walked around on the roof of the palace. From the roof he saw a woman bathing. The woman was very beautiful, and David sent someone to find out about her. The man said, "She is Bathsheba, the daughter of Eliam and the wife of Uriah the Hittite." Then David sent messengers to get her. She came to him, and he slept with her.

What's happening here?

David is in bed in the evening; some translations say, "in the afternoon." So that's idleness, not industry.

David is on his own not with his mighty men. That's isolationism rather than unity, and when we are isolated, we are easy prey.

Two out of the seven values we have been looking at in this book had been compromised already: industry and unity.

Now the process of temptation begins. Here is how the Apostle James describes this process in James 1:15-16 (The Passion Translation): *Evil desires give birth to evil actions. And when sin is fully mature it can murder you! So, my friends, don't be fooled by your own desires!*

David's fall begins with evil desires. When he should have been looking at his enemy on a battlefield, he was watching a woman having a bath. Desire began to entice him. Level 1 of the process of temptation accordingly begins with **enticement**. You can stop the process right there. Every man is tempted like this from time to time. But as the old saying goes, "you can't stop the birds flying over your head, but you can stop them nesting in your beard!"

David allows the birds to nest in his beard.

When these evil desires are not put to death, they give birth to evil actions. This is exactly what happens in David's case. He doesn't hesitate. He sends one of his servants to find out who the woman is. When they return, the tell the king her name, revealing in the process that she is married to Uriah. The matter should have stopped right there. But it doesn't. David sends the servant back with a message that she is required in the king's palace. At this point, the second phase in the tragedy begins: **entrapment**.

As soon as David has had sex with Bathsheba, the third phase starts: the phase of **enslavement**. The Apostle James calls this "death." When desires give way to deeds, deeds lead to death. In David's case, the death is literal, not just figurative. David's strength now becomes his weakness. His great strength (or one of them) was strategy, tactics, schemes for overcoming his enemies in battle. His great weakness was to use this same skillset to ensure that Uriah – Bathsheba's husband - is killed. That's death right there.

We can see here the third phase in David's downfall. His desires have mastered him. Instead of managing his own passions, he has submitted to them. When a leader cannot lead himself, he cannot lead his people. Now David's life disintegrates. He cannot stop himself from hurtling towards disaster. He has given in to enticement. He has become a victim of entrapment. Now he is powerless in a state of enslavement. This is how 2 Samuel 11 ends: *When Uriah's wife heard that her husband was dead, she mourned for him. After the time of mourning was over, David had her brought to his house, and she became his wife and bore him a son. But the thing David had done displeased the LORD* (vv. 26-27).

This divine displeasure was to lead to further death. The death of David and Bathsheba's firstborn son. Only when the prophet Nathan unveiled David's sins would this tide of darkness begin to be reversed.

[Diagram: a circular cycle showing ENTICEMENT (DESIRES) → ENTRAPMENT (DEEDS) → ENSLAVEMENT (DEATH)]

The Integrity Gap

From this moment on, David struggles day and night with something he's not encountered before – the gulf between the man of God he is in public and the man of sin he knows himself to be in private. This is what we mean by "the integrity gap." John Maxwell has some helpful things to say here. He describes the difference between the image we present to the world and the person we really are. "Image is what people think we are. Integrity is what we really are." A great gap – no, a yawning chasm has opened between David's image and his integrity, between his public persona and his private personality. As men of God, we must take great care not to let this happen. When there is a divorce between the public and the private, we start wearing masks, and when we start wearing masks, we become religious hypocrites.

C.S. Lewis once wisely remarked, "integrity is doing the right thing, even when no one is watching." When we cease to do the right thing, our public face may remain confident, but our private face will be tormented. We will look like we're still rowing, but our hearts will no longer be in it and we will be going through the motions, pretending rather than performing in the galley of the Lord. This is the pathway to inner pain.

David's agony at this point is expressed in one of the greatest songs of worship ever written, Psalm 51. It is the cry of repentance that rises from his heart when he knows that his integrity gap has been found out, through the warnings given by Nathan the prophet (1 Samuel 12).

> *God, give me mercy from your fountain of forgiveness!*
> *I know your abundant love is enough to wash away my guilt.*
> *Because your compassion is so great,*
> *take away this shameful guilt of sin.*
> *Forgive the full extent of my rebellious ways,*
> *and erase this deep stain on my conscience.*
> *For I'm so ashamed.*
> *I feel such pain and anguish within me.*
> *I can't get away from the sting of my sin against you, Lord!*
> *Everything I did, I did right in front of you, for you saw it all.*
> *Against you, and you above all, have I sinned.*

Millions of Christian men over the last two thousand years have had cause to get on their knees and pray this same prayer. When we fail or fall, we can either stay in the dust of the earth or rise to become men of glory again. Rising takes courage – the courage to be real, authentic, vulnerable and transparent. Indeed, as my friend Mark Stibbe has said, "it takes far greater bravery to rise up than it does stupidity to fall down."

David is being courageous here. He's being honest before God. He's revealing his whole heart. He's not hiding, he's disclosing. He's bringing his integrity gap to the feet of his Deliverer and his Saviour

CHAPTER 6 | MINDING THE GAP

God. He's trusting in God's unfailing mercy and his steadfast kindness. He's being real before his Lord, saying, "I'm fed up with this gap between my public self and my private self. I'm in agony of soul. Please forgive me, Oh God!"

Let me tell you something: God LOVES this kind of praying. He hates it when people put on a religious face, like the Pharisees did in Jesus' day. He loves it when people reveal their true selves, with all the hurts and hang-ups and habits we hide from one another. Remember the story Jesus told about the Pharisee and the publican. The publican came before God and wept over his sins. The Pharisee knelt and said how grateful he was that he wasn't like the publican.

That was an epic error of judgment.

It turns out that God wanted him to be like the publican!

He wants us all to be like the publican.

Real, not religious.

Honest, not hypocritical.

Sorrowful, not self-righteous.

God loves this.

As David says at the end of Psalm 51,

The fountain of your pleasure is found
in the sacrifice of my shattered heart before you.
You will not despise my tenderness
as I humbly bow down at your feet.

When Repentance is Real

Sometimes we do give way to enticement. This is tragic because it *always* has negative consequences for our lives. When we stop rowing and get off the galley, we can't expect there to be anything other than harmful effects when we take a holiday from commitment, a break from single-minded devotion to the Lord. When this happens, we need three things to happen if we are to reverse the process and get back on board with God's purpose.

Firstly, we need **a change of mind**. In other words, we need to look at what we've done from a different perspective, God's perspective. We can no longer justify our actions. We must own them. We must take responsibility for them, seeing them for what they are – what James calls *evil actions*. Until we stop treating evil as some sort of good, we will not be able to get back in the gallery and row. We must change the way we look at what we've done. We must have a Holy Spirit-inspired awakening and reality check.

Secondly, we need **a change of heart**. We must get to the point where we grieve over our sins. Remember Peter's restoration in John 21? The breakthrough comes when he is grieved at what Jesus says to him, when he gets in touch with his true feelings. He is no longer emotionally disengaged. He is showing godly sorrow. This is what we must do too; we must weep not because we have been found out but because we are genuinely sorry. As Paul writes:

The kind of sorrow God wants us to experience leads us away from sin and results in salvation. There's no regret for that kind of sorrow. But worldly sorrow, which lacks repentance, results in spiritual death (2 Corinthians 7:10, New Living Translation).

Godly sorrow is lifechanging.

Worldly sorrow is soul-destroying.

Thirdly, we need **a change of behaviour**. The fruit of genuine repentance is that we stop doing whatever is wrong (unrighteous) and we start doing what is right in the sight of God (righteousness). Instead of walking down the broad road to destruction, we take a U-turn and head back to the crossroads, choosing instead to walk along the narrow road to salvation. This narrow road is the road of integrity. It is the road travelled by the pure of heart.

A great example of this is Chuck Colson, one of President Nixon's righthand men known as "the hatchet man". When the Watergate

CHAPTER 6 | MINDING THE GAP

affair exposed corruption at the highest levels, Colson was convicted of obstructing justice and sent to prison. There he met Jesus, repented of his sin and was born again. Many people, especially in the press, accused Colson of faking it, describing his alleged spiritual experience as a sham. But when he was released, Colson proved that he had had a change of mind and a change of heart by the change in his behaviour. He created the Prison Fellowship Ministry, dedicated to working with prisoners, ex-prisoners and their families – a ministry that operates in 1300 prisons and works with over 7000 churches in the USA alone.

That's what God calls repentance.

A change of mind, a change of heart and a change of behaviour.

And repentance leads to restoring integrity.

This restoration of integrity in his private life was vital in David's case because he was the leader of an entire nation. Confucius once said that "the strength of a nation derives from the integrity of the home." Being the real deal in his own home, in his private world, was going to be essential not only for David but for the nation of Israel. Once integrity was restored, the nation could be built. While the integrity gap existed, everything was on hold.

The Beauty of Forgiveness

When David repented, God forgave him totally, instantly and unconditionally. This is what we are promised in the Bible. When we truly repent, God no longer holds our sins against us. The charges against us are dropped in heaven. God removes our sins as far from us as the east is from the west. And most remarkable of all, God remembers our sins no more. He forgets that we have done what we have done. The slate is wiped clean at the foot of the Cross. Our sins, which were as scarlet, are now as white as snow. Our filthy rags of unrighteousness are exchanged for the V.I.P robe given to the repentant, prodigal son. As we trust in the finished work of the Cross, we are justified – and justified, as Billy Graham used to say, means "just-as-if-I'd-never-sinned."

How do I know this is true?

Look at David's epitaph. When Paul the Apostle came to write the epitaph of David's life, he wrote: "David served God's purpose in his generation, and then he fell asleep." No mention of adultery there. No mention of murder either. God's summary of David's life is not a tragedy, it's a eulogy. His moral fall is not mentioned. Why? Because David was repented and was restored. It was "just-as-if-he'd-never-sinned!"

This is glorious news, especially for those who feel they have messed up so badly there can be no forgiveness and no fresh start. What happened after David and Bathsheba repented, after they had paid the price of their sins? God gave them another son. They named him Solomon. Solomon was "the son of David." Guess who was called "Son of David" a thousand years later? Jesus was! Why do you think Jesus accepted this title? It's because he knew that even though the original son of David (Solomon) was the child of David and Bathsheba, David and Bathsheba had repented before God. Therefore, it was "just-as-if-they'd-never-sinned". Therefore, he could accept the title joyfully.

And there's more. We focus often on David's repentance and restoration, and the consequences of that in the future of Israel. The Messiah, after all, was to come from the House of David. But there was another, Bathsheba, whose repentance and restoration were just as real and just as momentous in terms of long-term impact. She too was forgiven totally, instantly and unconditionally. For her too, it was "just-as-if-she'd-never-sinned!"

How do I know?

I know because in the Genealogy of Matthew (Matthew chapter 1), the ancestry of Jesus, Matthew mentions Bathsheba! He mentions four women, and that alone is radical. A Jewish writer like Matthew would normally have only recorded the male ancestors of a man like Jesus. In highlighting four women, Matthew highlights that the

Good News about Jesus brings honour and dignity not just to men but to women too.

The fact that Matthew includes a woman who had been a sex worker (Rahab) and a woman who had committed adultery (Bathsheba) shows how powerful it is when people repent. The goodness of this repentance doesn't just affect people now. It reverberates down the generations. And it's something so thrilling in the Father's eyes that when it came to the genealogy of his Son, God was pleased to have names like Rahab and Bathsheba in his family tree!

This, then, is the beauty and the glory of God's forgiveness. We are no longer defined by our failure. Heaven is a culture of honour and the hosts of heaven honour us again. On earth, people may still label us and say, "that's David, he committed adultery and murder." "That's Bathsheba, she was a marriage-breaker and a home-wrecker." But when people like this repent, these failures are edited out of our life story. They are remembered no more. There is no mention of them. The epitaph reads, "David served God's purpose", not "David broke the Ten Commandments".

Hallelujah for that!

Prevention, not just Cure

It has rightly been said, and in many different contexts, that prevention is better than cure. This is especially true when it comes to integrity. Men of God must seek to do everything within their power to find out where their weaknesses are and take steps to protect themselves from falling into sin.

In all this, accountability is vital. When Billy Graham established his four rules, he did so with the men with whom he shared his ministry. He didn't seek to go it alone in the fight for holiness. He had a band of brothers and they kept short accounts with each other. We need to learn from this.

As rowers in God's galley, we need to encourage one another, motivating each other to even higher levels of single-minded devotion, cheering each other on to greater degrees of integrity, remembering that "the supreme quality for leadership is unquestionably integrity. Without it, no real success is possible, no matter whether it is on a section gang, a football field, in an army, or in an office" (Dwight D. Eisenhower).

Billy Graham became more and more passionate about integrity in the years after the Modesto Manifesto was decided. He called older men in the church to become men of integrity, not least so that younger men could grow in holiness. As he said, "Integrity is the glue that holds our way of life together. What our young people want to see in their elders is integrity, honesty, truthfulness, and faith. What they hate most of all is hypocrisy and phoniness."

Billy also helped others himself in achieving higher levels of holiness. On one occasion, a young Christian man wrote him a letter about a challenge he was experiencing in the workplace. "I think I'm about to lose my job," he wrote. "Several weeks ago, my boss told me to do something that was clearly unethical (and probably illegal), and I told him that as a Christian, I couldn't do it. Was I wrong to refuse? He's been very cold to me ever since." Billy's reply is so insightful and revealing.

"No, you weren't wrong to refuse to do this. Even if you end up paying a stiff price for your integrity, God won't abandon you, and He will reward you for your faithfulness. The Bible says, 'Whoever walks in integrity walks securely, but whoever takes crooked paths will be found out' (Proverbs 10:9). Suppose you had gone along with what your boss wanted you to do. What would be the outcome? For one thing, almost certainly this would not have been the end; he would keep coming back to you with more and more unethical demands. In addition, if your involvement in these actions ever became known, your name would be dishonoured, and you could even be subject to legal action or arrest." He concluded, "Never compromise your integrity for a temporary gain!"

CHAPTER 6 | MINDING THE GAP

Integrity and Legacy

A good friend of mine, Pastor Chris Vigil from Reno, Nevada once said to me "Integrity is doing the right thing in every season of your life." That's so true. One of the marks of maturity for the man of God in the galley is the ability to preserve our integrity in the valleys as well as the peaks of life. That's not easy.

I have had the opportunity in many seasons and areas to deviate from integrity as a man, to get even and fight fire with fire, especially regarding relationships. In one such instance I experienced a very difficult three-year period of my life and everything I believed in, and walked in, was challenged. In this moment, I stood alone; the closest to me could not help and in this moment, I had the chance to seize the opportunity of a lifetime in the lifetime of the opportunity - to learn the way of the cross, the way of our saviour, to not compromise my integrity even though everything inside of me demanded justice and truth.

The opportunity came to embrace the fellowship of his suffering (Philippians 3:10), to not compromise my walk and talk with Christ for a moment of vengeance, to hold my integrity in Christ and trust his grace to empower me to walk through the valley of the shadow of death. Now, at the other end of this season, I have tasted a richer grace and greater mercy of Christ than I had ever experienced before. I'm so thankful that in the opportunity of a lifetime, the grace of Christ enabled me to seize the moment, bow my knee and let his mercy uphold me and set me free. This is walking in integrity.

Remember, there was no deceit (crookedness or bent nature) found in Christ. "He committed no sin, neither was deceit found in his mouth" (1 Peter 2:22). Integrity is a state of being whole and undivided, just as Christ was and is. Integrity is completeness, togetherness, integration between our talk and our walk, our public and our private life, between our orthodoxy (right believing) and our orthopraxy (right behaving).

Integrity is Jesus, and Jesus is integrity.

The lesson of integrity is one that King David learned the hard way. In his Psalms, he said,

"The very essence of your words is truth" (Psalm 119:160).

"I know that you are pleased with me, for my enemy does not triumph over me. Because of my integrity you uphold me and set me in your presence forever (Psalm 41:11-12, NIV)."

His son Solomon was to say this too:

"The godly walk with integrity; blessed are their children who follow them" (Proverbs 20:7, NLT).

No one who gets in the galley and rows can do without integrity.

As Billy Graham's story shows, when we mind the integrity gap, we seize our destiny, finish the race well, and leave a tremendous legacy. "Blessed are their children!"

What could be more fulfilling than that?

My friends, it's time to get in the galley and row!

> **QUOTE**
> *No man, for any considerable period, can wear one face to himself and another to the multitude, without finally getting bewildered as to which may be the true.*
>
> **Nathaniel Hawthorne**

CHAPTER 6 | MINDING THE GAP

QUESTIONS

1. Are you the same person in public as you are in private?

2. Are you regularly minding the integrity gap in your life?

3. What are the areas in your life where you need to grow in accountability?

4. How does your life measure up against the "Billy Graham Rule"?

5. Do you need to repent of anything right now?

6. What practical steps can you take to prevent yourself from becoming entrapped by sin in the future?

7. Are you modelling a life of integrity to the next generation?

THE 7 VALUES OF THOSE WHO GET IN THE GALLEY AND ROW

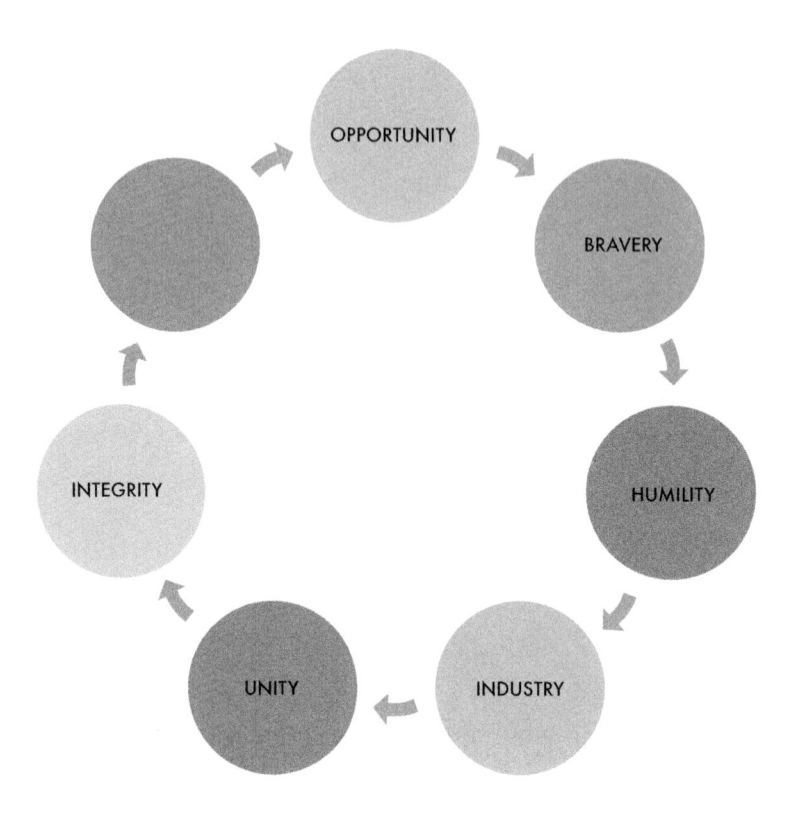

- OPPORTUNITY
- BRAVERY
- HUMILITY
- INDUSTRY
- UNITY
- INTEGRITY

CHAPTER 7

SOMEONE ABOVE DECKS

There are few Christian men who have carried a greater sense of destiny than Winston Churchill. By "destiny", I mean the sense that we are somehow predestined or foreordained by God for some great act or acts that will make a difference for good in our world. Using the language of Acts 13:38, having a sense of destiny means possessing a deep awareness that we are called to serve a specific purpose of God that is unique to our generation. Winston Churchill, the greatest war leader in British history, had this presentiment of God-given destiny. He had it embedded in his soul from an early age.

Even while he was still a boy, Churchill knew that God was calling him to a great purpose in his generation. When he was very young, he would wander around the ground floor rooms of Blenheim Palace and look up at the huge painting on the ceilings depicting his ancestor, the Duke of Marlborough, winning the Battle of Blenheim. He would stare at these vivid and detailed murals and sense that he too would one day rise to be a leader in a time of dangerous national conflict, that he too would be responsible for defeating the nation's enemies in a time of thick and increasing darkness.

When Churchill was just sixteen and a schoolboy at Harrow, he said these words: "Great upheavals, terrible struggles, wars such as one cannot imagine and I tell you, London will be in danger. London will be attacked, and I shall be very prominent in the defence of London. I shall be in command of the defences of London and I shall save London and England from disaster. Dreams of the future are blurred. But the main objective is clear, I repeat, London will be in danger and in the high position I shall occupy, it will fall to me to save the capital and save the empire." That is a very specific word of prophecy!

What is extraordinary about this is the one simple fact that at the time there was nothing at all to suggest that London would be in great danger and that England would need saving from disaster. This was 1891 and the British Empire was thriving, and the nation was prospering. Yet, in under fifty years, Churchill's prophetic words had been fulfilled. Promoted from the back to the front benches, from the Admiralty to the roll of Prime Minister, Churchill did indeed lead the country away from disaster, London included.

In a recent book (*Churchill: Walking with Destiny*, 2018), Andrew Roberts describes Churchill as "a man of destiny." He points out the number of times that Churchill could easily have died:

- He was born two months premature
- He was stabbed as a schoolboy
- He survived four bouts of pneumonia, one that nearly killed him as a child
- He survived three serious car crashes
- He fought in five wars in four continents as a soldier
- He ventured 30 times into No Man's land in the WW1 trenches
- He survived three plane crashes
- He survived a 30-feet fall from a bridge
- He walked out of a house that burned down in the middle of the night
- He was very nearly drowned in Lake Geneva
- He survived a series of strokes and heart attacks

As Andrew Roberts concludes, "Churchill became certain that the number of times he had narrowly escaped death meant he was a

CHAPTER 7 | SOMEONE ABOVE DECKS

man of destiny whose being saved for great things."

Two things should encourage us here. Firstly, the fact that Churchill was an ordinary, unspectacular boy and young man. He was an ordinary person destined by God to seize an extraordinary destiny. If you feel like a nobody, you're in good company. God selects nobodies and turns us into somebodies. Hitler regarded him as a hopeless has-been. The devil underestimates us to his cost!

The second thing that should encourage us is the fact that Churchill's sense of destiny was inexorably connected to his Christian faith. In his early years, the young Winston was an agnostic, but later he came to believe personally in God. That this came from a faith that was Christian and personal is beyond doubt. During these same years, he told Field Marshal Montgomery, "Jesus Christ was unsurpassed in his capacity to save sinners." It was this faith that drove Churchill to seize his destiny. As he said, "I felt as if I were walking with destiny, and that all my past life had been but a preparation for this hour and for this trial... I thought I knew a good deal about it all, I was sure I should not fail."

Above Decks

When Paul says of David that he served the purpose of God in his generation, this involved six things:

1. Opportunity

David was prepared to seize the opportunity of a lifetime in the lifetime of that opportunity. So did Winston Churchill. How about you?

2. Bravery

David was prepared to stand up and be counted, even when it came to facing giants. So was Churchill. How about you?

3. Humility

David was prepared to be humble and serve other leaders

behind the scenes during his years of leadership formation. So was Churchill. How about you?

4. Industry

David was prepared to work hard and tirelessly in the greater cause that he served. So was Churchill. How about you?

5. Unity

David was prepared to row in unity with others to serve God's purpose, and to call upon the nation to be united. So was Churchill. How about you?

6. Integrity

David was prepared to mind the gap between his private life and his public face. So was Churchill. How about you?

7. Destiny

David was prepared to serve God's unique purpose in his unique generation. So was Churchill. How about you?

One of the keys to David fulfilling his destiny was his faith. He served as an under-rower. That means he served below decks. When you're below decks, you can't see what's going on above you. You can't see the lookouts or hear what they are saying. You can't see or hear what the commander of the ship is observing nor what he is saying above decks. Being below decks involves faith. It demands that you believe that there is someone above you that you cannot see, someone who has the capacity to watch everything you can't watch, someone who has your best interests at heart. David had this quality. As it says in Hebrews 11:1-2 (The Message): *The fundamental fact of existence is that this trust in God, this faith, is the firm foundation under everything that makes life worth living. It's our handle on what we can't see. The act of faith is what distinguished our ancestors, set them above the crowd…* In verse 32, the writer mentions David as a champion of faith. David believed there was someone above decks whom he couldn't see: Almighty God!

CHAPTER 7 | SOMEONE ABOVE DECKS

Winston Churchill had this too.

During WW2, Churchill and his bodyguard narrowly escaped being killed by a falling bomb. Churchill turned to his companion and told him not to worry. Pointing to the sky, he said to him, "There's someone up there who has a mission for me to perform and He intends to see that that mission is performed."

Churchill had faith that there was someone above decks that had predestined him for a specific purpose. He knew that there was unfulfilled prophecy in his life. This trust in God was the firm foundation for his life and the key to serving God's purpose.

How about you?

David's Four Tasks

When we look in more detail at what David achieved in his lifetime, we can see that there were at least four main ways which David served the purposes of God in his generation and fulfilled God's will by faith2:

1. He unified a nation, a people

Before David's kingship, the twelve tribes of Israel had been held together as a loose alliance. In 2 Samuel 5, we read that the elders of these tribes - who held David in high esteem - came together and chose David as their leader. From there on, King David was able to accomplish something that had eluded King Saul; he unified the tribes of Israel. "When all the elders of Israel had come to King David at Hebron, the king made a covenant with them at Hebron before the Lord, and they anointed David king over Israel" (2 Samuel 5:3).

2. He established Jerusalem as the city of God

We read in 1 Chronicles 11:5 that David took the stronghold of Zion. Joab went up first and took the city and became chief as it was a strong fortress occupied by a Canaanite tribe, the Jebusites (Judges 1:21). Although David was anointed king in Hebron (2 Samuel

5:3), he established the walled city of Jerusalem as the capital of his kingdom. This was one of David's greatest accomplishments as king and one of the first actions he took as ruler of Israel. To this day, Jerusalem remains Israel's most sacred and holy city. And it was in this city that Jesus was crucified and to which He will one day return - the city of David, Jerusalem.

3. He brought the Ark to Jerusalem

Although it is King David's son, Solomon, who builds Israel's first temple, King David brings the "ark of God," or the Ark of the Covenant to Jerusalem. The Ark was the most significant object in Old Covenant worship. It was a box - overlaid with gold - in the Most Holy place. "A golden urn holding the manna, Aaron's staff that budded, and the tablets of the covenant" were placed within the Ark. The mercy seat covered the box. Two cherubim, facing one another, overshadowed the mercy seat. When God came down, His glory rested above the mercy seat - between the cherubim. The ark of covenant was designed to be a symbol of the presence of God in the midst of His people. King David placed God and worship back at the centre of Israel's hearts and minds by moving the ark into Jerusalem and it was during this time many of his Psalms, as well as the plans to build the Temple, began to emerge.

4. He established an inheritance for generations to come

After bringing the Ark of the Covenant back to Jerusalem, and David had started longing for a permanent place for the Ark to rest, the word of the Lord came to Nathan the prophet. In 2 Samuel 7:16 he told David that "Your house and your kingdom will endure forever before me; your throne will be established forever." One thousand years later, and out of David's line, came the messiah, Jesus. Not only did King David successfully rule over a unified Israel, but his reign also established a powerful dynasty. His offspring would be blessed for generations to come.

These are the four principal ways in which David served God's purpose before he fell asleep. These were the four building blocks of his unique destiny. For David, the most important thing was to do God's will while he was alive on the earth. Oh, how I love King David. He was a man after God's own heart who would do all His will (Acts 13:22).

We too can follow David's example in these four tasks, even if our specific purpose is different from his.

We can (1) be a force for unity in our home and in our church, making a resolution to avoid division and to foster the *homothumadon* principle – being of one heart and mind, in our families and churches.

We can (2) work to establish the church as the city of God, where songs and prayers of worship ascend night and day to heaven, treasuring and serving the local church as the dwelling place of God in every community.

We can (3) be carriers of the presence of God, bringing the Ark of the glory and fragrance of Christ into our families, churches and communities, with our hearts being the place where God's glorious presence resides.

We can (4) establish an inheritance for the generations to come, through our children (Proverbs 13:22), and through the people we disciple throughout the nations (Matthew 28:18-20).

Although there are tasks that are unique to our destiny, we can all follow David's example in these four areas. I believe a true man's vocation is that He is set apart as "the servant of God in the age in which he is born." Let's like David serve our own generation by the will of God. Let's put ourselves in the deepest galley of the ship and row with all our might and effort and heart and serve our generation and the generations to come with the will of God.

Time for Bed

Paul says that David served God's purpose in his generation, and then he *fell asleep*. Sleep here is another way of describing death.

From a Christian perspective, dying is not something to be feared. It is simply falling asleep at the end of a life lived for God. When a person comes to the end of their lives as an under-rower, they believe that there is someone above decks whom they cannot see, someone who will carry them home to the Father's house where they will wake on the Last Day. That is a very hopeful and beautiful picture.

Each one of us is called to serve God before we fall asleep. In our generation, there's one calling that we all share and that is to bring the Good News of Jesus to people all over the world. I have stood in the villages and mountain passes of Nepal and India, the cobbled streets Bath, London and the hamlets of England, the dust covered roads of Africa, the bright city lights of America and the war-torn fields of eastern Europe and the Middle East. In every context, I have found and seen the broken, lonely and bruised. I have seen God's healing come and I have seen it continue to come to the nations. It's time to arise and bring hope through the good news of Jesus Christ. Will we go? Will we heed the call and serve God's purpose?

If you are thinking, "I'm not called" at this point, think again. Remember what William Booth, founder of the Salvation Army, said in response to people who thought this way.

"Not called!" did you say?

"Not *heard* the call," I think you should say.

Put your ear down to the Bible and hear Him bid you go and pull sinners out of the fire of sin. Put your ear down to the burdened, agonized heart of humanity, and listen to its pitiful wail for help. Go stand by the gates of hell and hear the damned entreat you to go to their father's house and bid their brothers and sisters and servants and masters not to come there. Then look Christ in the face - whose mercy you have professed to obey - and tell Him whether you will join heart and soul and body and circumstances in the march to publish His mercy to the world."

We are all called. At a very general level, we all share the same

CHAPTER 7 | SOMEONE ABOVE DECKS

purpose or destiny. We are called to be conformed to the image of Christ and to bring his Good News to others. At a more specific level, we all have a unique purpose or destiny, and it is incumbent on all of us to find out what that is and then fulfil it during our lifetimes.

Then, and only then, can we fall asleep.

So, as I finish, let me close with a quotation from the great A.W. Tozer (1897-1963), whose writings on the spiritual life of the Christian are still relevant to this day. He said this:

"To fall asleep before we have served our generation is nothing short of tragic. It is good to sleep at last, as all our honoured fathers have done, but it is a moral calamity to sleep without having first laboured to bless the world. No man has any right to die until he has put mankind in debt to him. No man has any moral right to lie down on the earth till he has wrought to take something of the earth out of the hearts of men, till he has helped to free men from the tyranny of that same earth and pointed them to that kingdom that will abide after the heavens and the earth are no more."

My friends, it's time to get in the galley and row!

---

[2] For these four tasks, I'm indebted, among others to Nicholas Batzig. This is one of those situations where I've picked up the idea of the four Davidic purposes from different sources over a long period of my life. If you're one of them, let me know and I'll acknowledge it in the next edition.

> **QUOTE**
>
> *I don't know what your destiny will be, but one thing I know: the ones among you who will be truly happy are those who have sought and found how to serve.*
>
> Albert Schweitzer

CHAPTER 7 | SOMEONE ABOVE DECKS

QUESTIONS

1. In what ways, if at all, do you feel like you are walking with destiny?

2. Do you have a sense of what your unique, long-term destiny might look like?

3. In what ways is God calling you to serve his purpose in your generation?

4. Are you determined to fulfil God's purpose *before* you die?

5. Which of the seven values celebrated in this book do you need to work on?

6. How are you going to ensure that these values are always embedded and exhibited in your life?

7. Are you going to go on rowing in God's galley until your last breath?

THE 7 VALUES OF THOSE WHO GET IN THE GALLEY AND ROW

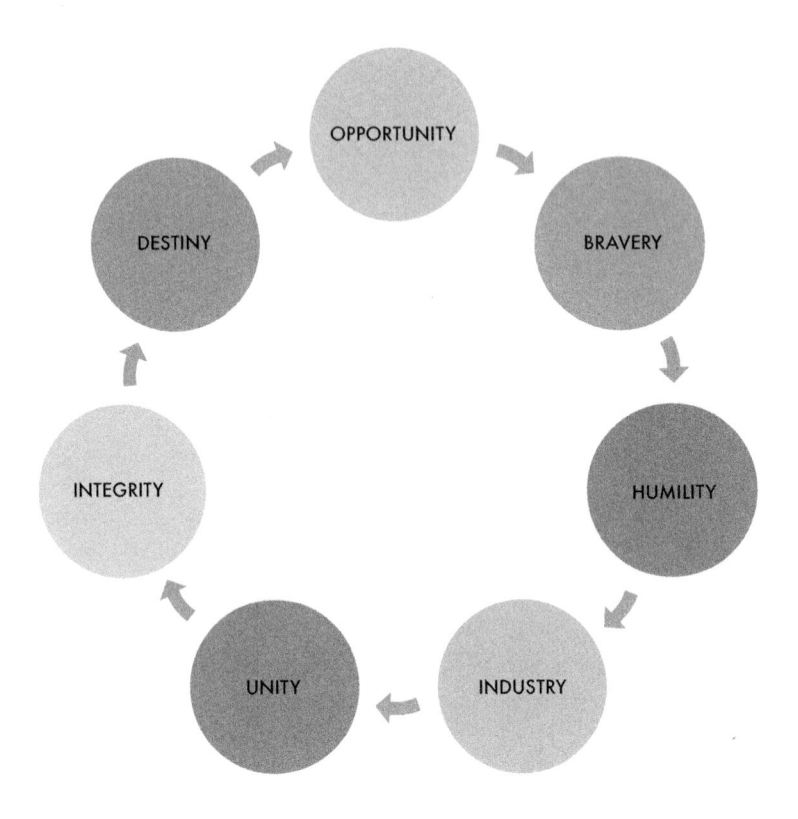

- OPPORTUNITY
- BRAVERY
- HUMILITY
- INDUSTRY
- UNITY
- INTEGRITY
- DESTINY